Sew a Dinosaur

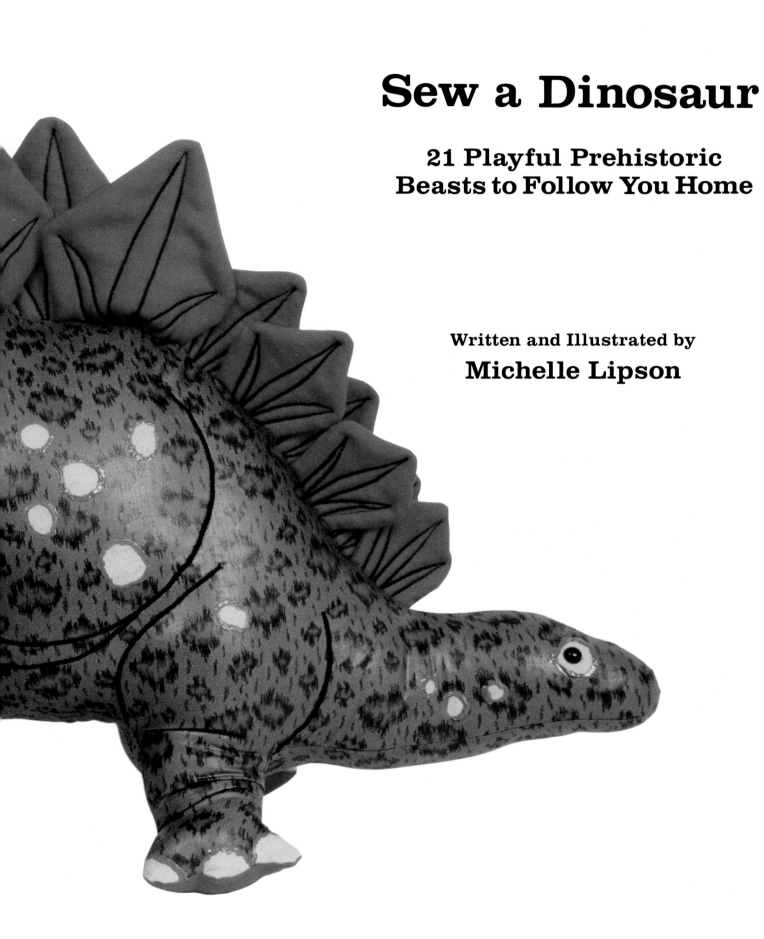

Sew a Dinosaur

21 Playful Prehistoric Beasts to Follow You Home

Written and Illustrated by

Michelle Lipson

A Sterling/**Lark** book

Sterling Publishing Co., Inc., New York

Dedicated to the memory
of my beloved father,
Leonard Lipson

Acknowledgements

Although I'm credited as the author and illustrator of this book, it could have never been written without the help of the following people:

My husband, John Pousson, and our children, Amelia, Eli, and Sophia; my mother, Lillian Lipson; my editor, Carol Taylor; and graphic artist Kimberley Ann Becker.

Each in his or her own special way made it possible for me to realize my dream of creating this book of dinosaurs. Thank you.

—Michelle Lipson

Editor: Carol Taylor
Design: Judy Clark and Rob Pulleyn
Production: Judy Clark and
      Elaine Thompson
Photography: Evan Bracken

Library of Congress Cataloging-in-
    Publication Data

Lipson, Michelle.
    Sew a dinosaur: 21 playful prehistoric
beasts to follow you home / by Michelle
Lipson.
      p.   cm.
    "A Sterling/Lark book."
    ISBN 0-8069-8212-8
    1. Soft toy making.
    2. Dinosaurs.   I. Title
TT174.3.L57   1990
745.592'4--dc20
                  90-45158
                  CIP

ISBN 0-8069-8212-8 Trade
ISBN 0-8069-8213-6 Paper

10 9 8 7 6 5 4 3 2 1

A Sterling/Lark Book

Produced by Altamont Press, Inc.
50 College Street, Asheville, NC 28801, USA

Published in paperback 1991 by Sterling
    Publishing Co., Inc.
387 Park Avenue South, New York, NY 10016

Copyright © 1991, Michelle Lipson

Distributed in Canada by Sterling Publishing
c/o Canadian Manda Group, P.O. Box 920,
    Station U
Toronto, Ontario, Canada M8Z 5P9

Distributed in Australia by Capricorn Link, Ltd.
P.O. Box 665, Lane Cove, NSW 2066

Contents

calvin and HOBBES
by WATTERSON

THIS IS SUPPOSED TO BE GREAT ART.

...SO WHY DOES IT LOOK LIKE A BUNCH OF DECAPITATED NAKED PEOPLE?

A STRANGE FEELING COMES OVER CALVIN IN THE ART MUSEUM.

HIS PARENTS, ENGROSSED IN CULTURE, REMAIN BLISSFULLY UNAWARE OF CALVIN'S TERRIBLE TRANSFORMATION!

YES, A TYRANNOSAURUS IS LOOSE IN THE ART MUSEUM! THE CURATOR SHRIEKS, AND PANDEMONIUM ENSUES!

A GUARD REACHES FOR HIS PISTOL, BUT THE DINOSAUR IS UPON HIM AND HE IS MESSILY DEVOURED!

THE GIANT LIZARD'S GLORY IS CAPTURED FOREVER ON FILM BY THE ANTI-THEFT CAMERAS! PATRONS OF THE ARTS FLEE FOR THEIR LIVES!

HUNDREDS OF PRICELESS PAINTINGS ARE RIPPED TO SHREDS IN THE AWFUL RAMPAGE! WEALTHY BENEFACTORS ARE TRAMPLED! THE MUSEUM IS IN RUINS! ON TO SYMPHONY HALL!!

CALVIN? ... CALVIN? WE'RE IN THE NEXT ROOM NOW. C'MON.

I THINK WE'D BETTER GET HIM OUT OF HERE. HE HAD THAT GRIN AGAIN.

I WANNA SEE THE DINOSAURS AT THE NATURAL HISTORY MUSEUM AGAIN.

WE SPENT ALL AFTERNOON THERE, CALVIN.

The assembled soft sculptures, wind toys, and puppets from later chapters.

Introduction

Triceratops was worn and his stuffing leaked, but he was my favorite. From the first day my mother gave him to me, "Three-Horned Face" was an important part of my life. With him under my arm, I could imagine real dinosaurs just beyond the trees, in a wonderland where Pteranodon soared, Tyrannosaurus Rex roared, and Baby Protoceratops was just being hatched.

I am grown now, but I still remember fondly those realistic yet cuddly and lovable toys she made for me. They were so important in the enchanted world of my imagination.

Triceratops, page 43

Ask a child or two for their favorite subject, and chances are that you will hear a quick shout of "Dinosaurs!" Few subjects intrigue the young and old as much as these wonderful dragons of the past. Even though they vanished from the face of the earth 65 million years ago, they continue to exert a magical fascination.

Only a decade ago, most people thought that dinosaurs were dull-colored, slow-moving, slow-witted lizards. The image of a typical specimen was Brontosaurus standing up to his knees in a vast swamp, next to a hairy caveman brandishing a huge club. During the last 10 or 15 years, however, scientists have been unraveling some of the mysteries surrounding these awesome reptiles and have changed the way we think about them. Brontosaurus has a new name, Apatosaurus—the result of a surprising discovery that the head found with the first Apatosaurus fossil was from another dinosaur entirely! Since the first hominid did not appear until a mere 3.5 million years ago, the caveman is gone from our picture too. Paleontologists now feel that the dinosaurs were a livelier group, faster and more agile, their colors brighter and more varied than was previously thought. Lovely greens, blues, and purples are the new palette of colors used by scientific illustrators to help us visualize the dinosaurs that roamed the earth for 180 million years.

Children are fascinated by these creatures from the distant past. For some it is the beginning of a lifelong interest in science and the world around them. Because children take their knowledge about dinosaurs very seriously, they are offended by a false dinosaur, one that is an amalgamation of dinosaur characteristics. They know exactly what their favorite looked like and will tell you so without any encouragement.

For this book I have attempted to create patterns that incorporate some of the new discoveries about dinosaurs. Accurate silhouettes, attention to proportion, and a concern with surface design all add up to some very realistic reptiles. I have also included patterns for some other prehistoric beasts that lived during the Age of Dinosaurs, such as the pterosaurs and some proto-dinosaurs.

You will find a variety of projects in this book. Some will sew together very quickly, while others will take more time. They are all guaranteed to please dinosaur lovers of all ages.

Protoceratops Hatchling, page 86

Beastly Biographies

Dinosaurs lived during the Mesozoic Era, from 245 to 65 million years ago. The first dinosaurs appeared during the early part of the era, known as the Triassic period. During the Jurassic period that followed— the middle of the Mesozoic Era— dinosaurs became very large, and sea reptiles and pterosaurs also evolved. There were lots of insects, lizards, salamanders, and small mammals as well. By the final part of the Mesozoic Era— the Cretaceous period—the earth began to look much as it does today, and the planet played host to flowering plants, birds, and dinosaurs. After the Cretaceous period, there were no pterosaurs, dinosaurs, or sea serpents left alive; they had vanished completely. One of the great scientific puzzles in the history of life on earth is the extinction of the dinosaurs.

Everything that we know about dinosaurs we have learned from fossils. Scientists study the remains of dinosaurs preserved in rock, found on every continent on earth, to learn about how dinosaurs ate and reproduced, looked and sounded. The first dinosaur fossil was found in 1674 in southern England—a piece of thigh bone from a Megalosaurus, a huge, meat-eating dinosaur that lived 100 million years ago.

Dinosaurs were named by Richard Owen, an English scientist, in 1841. After comparing dinosaur bones with those of modern animals, Owen decided that these prehistoric creatures were unlike any reptiles he knew. Convinced that they must have been very large, ferocious, and lizard-like, he combined two Greek words to name them: *deinos* and *sauros*, or "terrible lizards." Of course, today we know that they were not lizards and many of them were not terrible, or even very large. So far, 300 different kinds of dinosaurs have been discovered.

Dinosaurs came in many sizes and shapes. Some, such as Ultrasaurus, were huge, while others, such as Compsognathus, were smaller than a rooster. While many dinosaurs were meat-eaters, others were vegetarians. All lived on land. Some walked on their hind legs and some on all four.

Each pattern in this book contains a short biography of the beast. Because most dinosaurs have scientific names that are composed of either Greek or Latin words in combination, many of their names are hard to pronounce and difficult to spell. You will find phonetic spellings for each dinosaur in the pattern section.

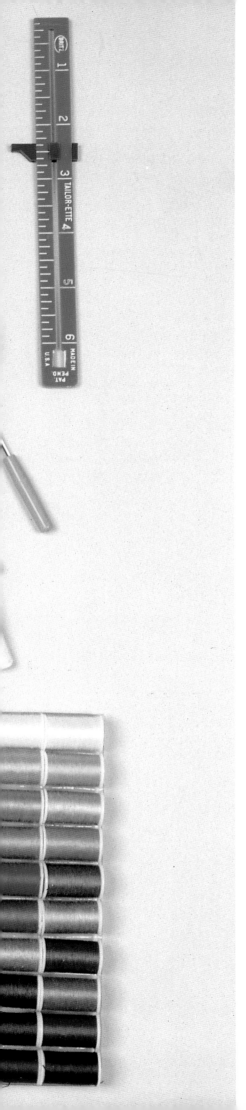

General Sewing Procedures

The sewing techniques for toy making are the same as those for dressmaking. If you are familiar with a sewing machine and carefully follow the instructions, you will be able to complete these dinosaurs in a professional manner, even if you've never stuffed a toy in your life.

This chapter provides a general explanation of basic sewing techniques. If you need more information, please refer to a basic sewing manual. (Several are listed in the bibliography.)

Before starting a project, read all instructions carefully, examining the pattern pieces as you read and trying to visualize each step. Take your time, work carefully, and, most important, have fun!

A Safety Reminder

When sewing a toy, it is important to consider the age of the child who is to receive it. Avoid small buttons and other embellishments that could become a choking hazard. If the toy is for a young and active child, use sturdy fabrics and double-stitch seams that will receive stress.

Tools

Check each pattern for a list of notions and fabrics before beginning construction. Otherwise, you will need only a sewing machine and some basic sewing suplies to construct these patterns.

Marking tools	Thimble
Tape measure	Iron
Pins	Thread
Scissors	Needles
Pincushion	Seam ripper

Preshrinking

Wash and dry the fabric, using the same techniques that you will use on the assembled dinosaur. This not only removes sizing and any chemicals that may still be in the fabric but also enables you to be more successful in cleaning the completed toy.

Ironing

Ironing is an essential part of sewing. Before you start, press the fabric on the wrong side, and use a cool setting to smooth paper patterns flat. As seams are sewn, they should be ironed open, if possible.

Pattern Markings

 **Cutting line.** Continuous solid line on the outer edge of the pattern.

 **Dart.** Fold on dot-dashed line, and stitch on dashed line.

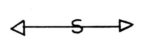 **Stitching line.** Dashed line; also used to indicate machine quilting.

 **Notches and circles.** For matching pattern pieces.

Grain line. Place on straight grain of fabric, parallel to selvage.

Stretch line. Greatest amount of stretch in knit fabric.

Fold line. A dot-dashed line.

Eye placement. A small circle with a plus sign.

Plastic joint placement. A large circle with an X.

Layout

Each pattern includes a cutting layout for 45″-wide fabric, which shows you exactly how to position and cut out the pieces of a pattern from the specified amount of fabric. Place all paper patterns on fabric according to illustrated layout. If you purchase a different width of fabric or you wish to use some scraps left from a previous project, you will have to do a trial layout. Lay your fabric on a table and move your pattern pieces around until you find the most efficient arrangement. Then proceed with pinning and cutting.

Remember to check the following:

Grain lines should be parallel to the selvage.

Be sure that you have all the pattern pieces before you start work; note carefully which pieces have multiple parts.

When *fold* is indicated on the layout, fold fabric with right sides together.

When using napped fabric, lay all pattern pieces in same direction, or the seams will be obvious. Nap should be running down the body.

Pinning

To insure accurate alignment of fabric when sewing, it is essential that the pieces be held firmly. Pins should be inserted approximately 2″ (5 cm.) apart at right angles to the seam. Keep the pin heads in the seam allowance area, so they can be removed easily as you sew.

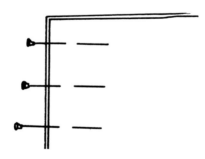

Cutting Fabric

Cut through the fabric and pattern on the cutting line. Cut accurately, making long, firm cuts, sliding the shears along to make the next cut while holding your other hand flat on the pattern piece, near the cutting line, for the smoothest edge. Cut notches outward and groups of notches in continuous blocks.

Cutting Foam

1. Cut out paper patterns for foam.
2. Place each pattern on foam sheet as shown on the layout for each project.
3. Hold pattern in place, and trace outline on foam with felt-tip marker.
4. Repeat for pieces requiring more than one foam layer, as noted.
5. Cut foam on inside of marked line.

Seam Allowance

Check individual pattern instructions for seam allowance (the distance between cutting line and seam line). A seam allowance is included in all patterns.

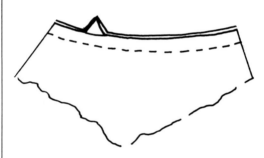

Transferring Markings

Before removing the pattern from the fabric, transfer all construction lines and symbols. Use chalk, tailor's tacks, a marking pen, or a tracing wheel and dressmaker's tracing paper.

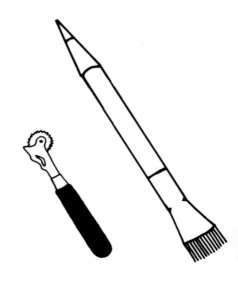

Seams

To make good strong seams, use quality thread, a new needle, and tightly spaced stitches. Place fabric pieces together, match notches, and position pins securely at right angles along the fabric edge. Baste if instructions indicate. To avoid hitting a pin with the sewing machine needle, remove pins as you stitch.

Easing

When two pieces to be joined are uneven in length, the longer must be eased to fit the shorter. Easestitch the longer on the seam line with a medium-large stitch. As you sew, force the material through the machine somewhat, which will pull up the fabric. Pin eased piece to other piece and stitch, eased side up.

Clipping

Clipping insures that curved seams will lie flat after the piece is turned right side out. Cut a short distance into the seam allowance with the point of the scissors, taking care not to cut into the stitching. Clip on outside curves and notch on inside curves.

Trimming

Trim seams by cutting off approximately half the seam allowance, following the line of stitching.

Turning

To turn pieces right side out, use a ¼″ (6 mm.) dowel or large tapestry needle.

Stitches

Baste. Long, even, running stitches used to join two fabrics temporarily.

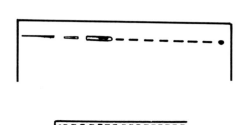

Edgestitch. A row of straight stitching applied very close to a finished edge, used to seam parts together. Similar to topstitching, which is done farther away from the edge—¼″ to ½″ (6 mm. to 12 mm.).

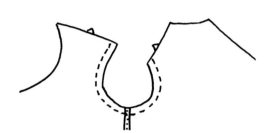

Staystitch. A line of machine stitching placed in the seam allowance close to the seam line. Staystitching stabilizes the area so it retains its shape.

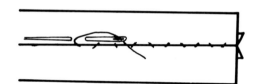

Slipstitch. A hand stitch used to join two folded edges of fabric. If worked carefully, slipstitches can be almost invisible. Use a strong thread to close openings of toys; carpet thread and buttonhole thread are both good choices.

Finishing

Inspect the project. Pins removed? Loose threads clipped? Seams tight?

Apatosaurus, page 39

Stuffing

A toy can be stuffed with any-thing soft, from rags to pantyhose and from sand to cornhusks. I strongly recommend polyester fiberfill. Lightweight, durable, and hypoallergenic, it is easy to work with, machine washable, and available at fabric and craft stores.

Toys look better if they are firmly stuffed. As a general rule, stuff a little bit at a time, using a dowel or chopstick to pack the stuffing firmly. Areas such as necks and legs should be solidly packed, as they tend to get soft after some really serious play. In some instances, you may wish to permanently insert a dowel into areas that are likely to get floppy, such as necks.

It's a good idea to let the stuffed toy rest overnight before you sew it closed. If you find that you can pack it fuller the next day, you should.

Enlarging Patterns

Since all the patterns have been reduced to fit the pages of this book, they must be enlarged to their original size. Each pattern has a legend that indicates by how much. If, for example, one square = 1″ (2.5 cm.), then each of the squares in the grid printed in the book represents 1″ of actual size in the pattern.

There are several ways to en-large patterns.

1. Use a photocopy machine with an enlarging capacity. En-large the pattern until you reach the appropriate size.

2. Use an opaque projector. Project the pattern onto a wall at the correct size, and trace the pattern on paper taped to the wall.

3. The pattern can be photo-stated to the scale given on the drawing. Check in your phone book for companies that do photo-stating.

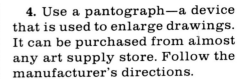

4. Use a pantograph—a device that is used to enlarge drawings. It can be purchased from almost any art supply store. Follow the manufacturer's directions.

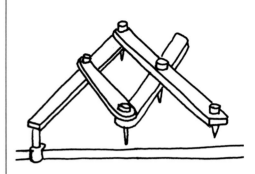

5. Lay out your own graph paper or purchase some with squares of the correct size. For example, if the legend says one square = 1″ (2.5 cm.), buy paper with a 1″ grid. Copy the pattern shapes from the smaller grid to the larger grid square by square. When all the lines are transferred, the enlarged pattern is ready to use. Be sure to transfer all the information that is on each pattern.

Choosing a Fabric

The fabric you select is very important. It will become, after all, your dinosaur's skin. As you consider different colors, tex-tures, and weights, think about the personality of your dinosaur. Was she a meat eater who preyed on smaller dinosaurs? Or was he a more placid type who existed on a vegetarian diet? Don't forget the new owner of your creation. Is this dinosaur destined to be the constant companion of a three-year-old or a decoration for a teenager's room? What kind of surface design do you plan to use—paint, needlework, or no-thing at all?

Allosaurus Sweatshirt, page 109

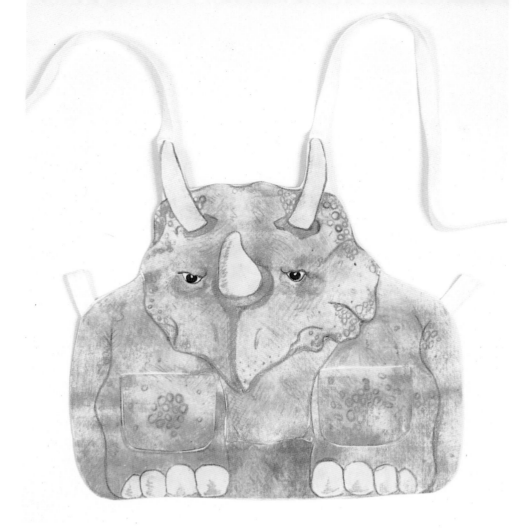

Triceratops Apron, page 113

Since no one is sure what color dinosaurs were, don't limit yourself to dull hues. These dragons could have been any color imaginable. For all we know, they were polka-dotted. All the fossil record can tell us is that their skin texture was much like that of modern reptiles.

If a specific type of fabric is necessary for the success of a project, the fabric recommendation for the pattern will say so. Otherwise, a wide variety of fabrics will serve. A medium-weight cotton or cotton blend is an excellent choice, since it is durable, comes in many colors, and accepts paints and dyes readily. In addition, it is easy to sew and press. Whatever fabric you choose, check on the procedure for washing.

To me, imitation fur looks very odd on a dinosaur. Fur says "mammal," and there is little debate in the scientific community that dinosaurs were reptiles. If you yearn for the soft feel of fur, consider corduroy, cotton velveteen, or a low-stretch velour.

Suggested Fabrics

Woven cotton and cotton blends	Percale
	Poplin
Broadcloth	Gabardine
Lightweight canvas	Sheeting
	Sateen
Denim	Velveteen
Duck	Corduroy

Cleaning

Whenever a child loves a toy very much, it is not surprising that the toy gets soiled. There are a few things you can do to keep the dirt level under control—and to launder it successfully.

1. Preshrink the fabric. If you skip this step, the toy may come apart when washed.

2. Treat the finished dinosaur with a soil-repellent spray.

3. Try to surface-clean the toy if possible.

4. When the dinosaur simply must have a bath, put it into a pillowcase, tie the case shut, and wash in warm or cold water with gentle action. Line dry.

The Projects

Before starting to sew, carefully read the instructions and assembly diagrams. *Visualize* each step. Do each step in the sequence noted.

1. Enlarge patterns.
2. Choose fabric.
3. Preshrink fabric.
4. Iron fabric and paper patterns.
5. Pin pattern pieces on fabric as shown on layout.
6. Cut pieces along solid line and around notches.
7. Transfer markings from paper patterns to fabric.
8. Repeat steps 5, 6, and 7 for polyester fiberfill batting and iron-on interfacing where applicable.
9. Apply surface design (optional). Any painting, printing, dyeing, or needlework that will work best with flat fabric should be done now.

Note: Some of the patterns in this book require that the surface design be applied even before the fabric is cut into pattern pieces. If you are going to sew one of these projects, change the order of the steps:

1. Enlarge patterns.
2. Choose fabric.
3. Preshrink fabric.
4. Iron fabric and paper patterns.
5. Transfer markings from paper patterns to fabric.
6. Apply surface design.
7. Pin pattern pieces on fabric as shown on layout.
8. Cut pieces along solid line and around notches.
9. Repeat pinning, cutting, and transferring steps for polyester fiberfill batting and iron-on interfacing where applicable.

Rating of Patterns

Some of the patterns in this book are quick and easy to sew, requiring a little over an hour from start to finish. Others take more time. In order to guide you, the following rating system will give you an approximate idea of sewing time.

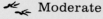 Fast and easy

Moderate

Extended project

Surface Design

Splashes of paint, bits of appliqué, judicious quilting, textured stamps, or delicate embroidery can transform ordinary fabric into just about anything—including dinosaur skin. Often the most exciting and creative part of a project, surface design can make your dinosaur come alive, a unique and individual image of a prehistoric beast.

Of course, you won't always need decoration. If you're like me, sometimes you'll be browsing in a fabric store looking for a certain color or texture, only to stumble upon a fabric that fairly screams "Dinosaur!" (You may be the only customer who can hear it.) Purchase the fantastic fabric and let it convey the image all by itself.

Basically, surface design techniques can be divided into paint and needlework. In this book, each project can use those techniques singly or in combination. In some cases, the surface design is an essential part of the pattern; other times it's optional. The kite pattern, for example, is an ordinary delta kite until the design is painted on. Many of the techniques are interchangeable, and you may decide to paint or crayon rather than embroider or appliqué. Allow your creativity to express itself. You should feel free to use your favorite technique on almost any of the projects. Take a moment before you begin a project to reflect on what techniques you wish to use. In many cases the surface design is best applied before any assembly is begun.

Be careful, however, because the surface design techniques described as part of the assembly instructions are frequently important to the structure of the dinosaur. The technique of machine quilting is often used to provide form to the fabric. If the technique is not important for structure, then it will be marked "Optional" and may be omitted.

I have recommended only those techniques of surface design for which the materials are widely available and which take little or no special equipment. In addition, I have paid special attention to insure that the techniques don't involve toxic fumes. More and more manufacturers are developing products that can be used without special ventilation, gloves, or solvents. There are a number of water-based paints and dyes for use on fabric which can be used safely within the home environment.

Remember: Carefully read the instructions for all products, and always use proper ventilation. Keep paints and dyes out of reach of children. Paints and fabric crayons specifically formulated for use by children are available; these are marked "nontoxic."

It is a wonderful experience for children to be presented with the opportunity of drawing or painting the dinosaur skin themselves. Given the chance, a child will enjoy taking part in the creative process, and dinosaurs made from this personally embellished fabric are frequently the most cherished and the most beautiful.

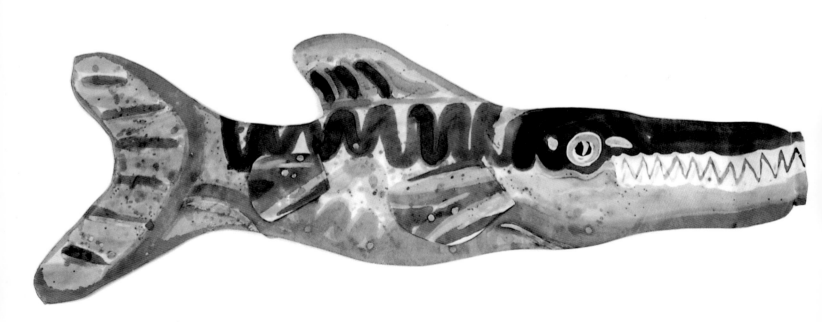

Ichthyosaurus Wind Sock, page 91

General Instructions for Using Paint on Fabric

Fabric paints are pigments suspended in a binder. The binder is the means by which the pigment (color) is held onto the fibers of the fabric. Fabric paints can be used on any fabric that has not been treated with a repellent finish.

Rhamphorhynchus

Sled Kite, page 94

1. Look for paints that are nontoxic and water-based (diluted or cleaned with water).

2. Wash, dry, and iron the fabric. Unexciting as this step may be, it's also important. If any sizing or starch remains in the fabric, the paint may adhere to it rather than to the fibers and may wash out at first laundering.

3. Decide whether the fabric can remain as yardage while the paint is applied, or must be cut into pattern pieces first. If you wish to apply an all-over design without any specific details such as eyes, mouth, or toes, then it will be fine to leave the fabric in one piece. To paint specific details of dinosaur anatomy, however, either trace the pattern onto the fabric or cut the pattern out before applying the paint.

If you are uncertain about where to locate painted details—toenails, for example—consider sewing and stuffing your dinosaur first. Then mark the correct locations and unstuff it. Put paper between the still-attached layers of fabric to prevent the paint from bleeding through, paint in the details, and restuff.

It isn't unusual for me to realize after a dinosaur is finished that it needs just a touch more paint in one or two places. So even though I have stuffed and closed the openings, I will paint the stuffed dinosaur. To set the paint, I carefully hold a steam iron above the painted areas.

4. Transfer your design to the fabric, using chalk (regular or tailor's), a water-soluble fabric marker, or even a soft pencil (you can paint over lead pencil marks).

5. Cover your work surface. Paint can be messy, and clean-up will be easier if you start with a layer of newspaper.

6. Test your paints on a scrap of fabric.

7. Refer to the directions for specific painting techniques later in this chapter, and apply the paint.

8. When the painting is completed, allow the fabric to dry completely. To set the paint, iron on the reverse side of the fabric, using a cotton setting. Then, using a piece of white paper to protect your iron, press on the front side of the fabric.

Fabric paints that air-dry do not need to be heat-set. Follow the manufacturer's instructions.

There are many wonderful and varied inks, dyes, and paints that work extremely well on fabric, even for the novice. I have described only some of the many techniques. You might want to be adventurous and try some paints, dyes, or inks that are not covered in this book.

Finally, don't limit yourself to painting on plain fabrics. Carefully applied paint can also enhance printed materials.

Brush Painting

Equipment

Watercolor or acrylic brushes, a variety of sizes

Fabric (use any of the suggested types)

Container of water (for washing brushes)

Fabric paints

Technique

1. Painting on fabric is much like painting on paper. You can produce precise lines with small brushes and flowing strokes with broad ones. Just dip your brush in the fabric paint, and begin. Be sure to wash your brush when you change colors.

2. Combine colors to create new ones as needed. To mix fabric paint follow the same rules as for other kinds. (For example, blue and yellow will yield green.)

3. Allow paint to dry overnight, or for about 12 hours.

4. Iron fabric on reverse side to set the paint.

Sponge Painting

Equipment

Household sponges

Fabric paints

Fabric

Technique

Direct method:

1. Wet sponge with water, and squeeze out excess moisture. Sponge should be damp.

2. Dip a small piece of sponge in fabric paint. Dab paint onto the fabric with a rolling motion. Lift and repeat.

3. Use a new sponge for each color, or clean your sponge when you change colors.

4. Allow paint to dry for 12 hours.

5. Iron on reverse side of fabric to set paint.

Indirect method:

1. Using scissors or a craft knife, cut sponge into the desired shape. Some craft stores sell sponges in a variety of basic shapes—letters and numbers, for example.

2. Dampen sponge, and squeeze out excess water.

3. With a paintbrush, apply paint to sponge.

4. Press sponge gently onto a piece of scrap paper, to remove excess paint.

5. Press sponge gently onto fabric.

6. Allow paint to dry for 12 hours.

7. Iron on reverse side of fabric to set paint.

Plastic Spray Bottle

Equipment

Plastic bottle with spray attachment

Fabric paint

Fabric

Technique

Fill bottle with paint and spray on fabric. You might want to experiment on a piece of newspaper first, to determine your optimum distance from the surface.

Splatter Painting

Equipment

Old toothbrush

Fabric paints

Fabric

Technique

1. You might want to practice your technique by splatter-painting a couple of pieces of newspaper before you let fly on the fabric. That way you'll have a good idea of how hard you have to tap to produce the amount of paint you want.

2. Dip a toothbrush in fabric paint. Gently tap the toothbrush against a finger to produce a splatter of paint on the fabric.

3. Repeat until you are pleased with the effect.

4. Repeat with additional colors until the dinosaur is also pleased.

5. Allow paint to dry for about 12 hours.

6. Iron on reverse side of fabric to set paint.

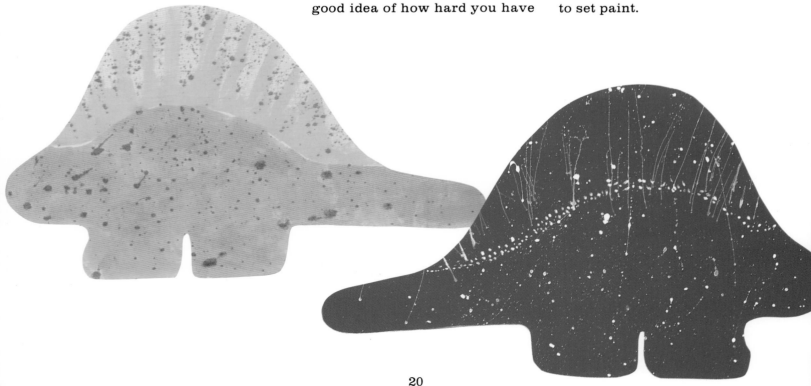

Dimensional Paint

Equipment

Paints in plastic squeeze bottles
Fabric

Technique

1. Some craft paints that come in plastic bottles are designed to be squeezed directly onto the fabric. Check the label to make sure that's what you've got. Thick, usually acrylic, ranging from shiny to puffy, these paints produce striking dimensional effects.

2. Remove the cap, place the bottle tip on the fabric, and squeeze gently, producing squiggles, dots, lines, or any other markings that cross your mind.

3. When you apply the paint lightly or in very fine lines, flex or stretch the fabric as you paint, to insure good adhesion to the fibers. This will eliminate the peeling and cracking that often occur if the piece is laundered repeatedly.

4. If this technique isn't (ahem) your main squeeze, try applying the paint with a brush or spatula.

5. While dimensional paint is easy on the artist, it wreaks havoc on a sewing machine needle, which unfailingly sticks in the paint and stretches it off the fabric. Avoid applying acrylic paints in areas that will be stitched later.

6. Allow the paint to set for about 12 hours.

7. Iron on reverse side of fabric to set paint. (Check the manufacturer's instructions.)

Stenciling

Equipment

Tracing paper

Rubber cement

Stencil paper

or

Mylar (available at art supply houses)

Craft knife

Stencil brush

Fabric paint

Fabric

Technique

1. If you're using tracing paper, trace the image onto the paper. With the rubber cement, glue the tracing paper drawing to the stencil paper.

2. If you're using Mylar, trace the image directly onto the Mylar sheet.

3. With craft knife, cut out the design areas that you wish to paint.

4. Place fabric on newspaper-covered surface, and lay stencil in position on the fabric. Tape stencil so that it does not move.

5. Dip brush into paint and, using a dabbing motion, apply paint to the cut-out areas of the stencil, working from the edges to the outside.

6. Allow paint to dry for about 12 hours.

7. Iron on reverse side of fabric to set paint.

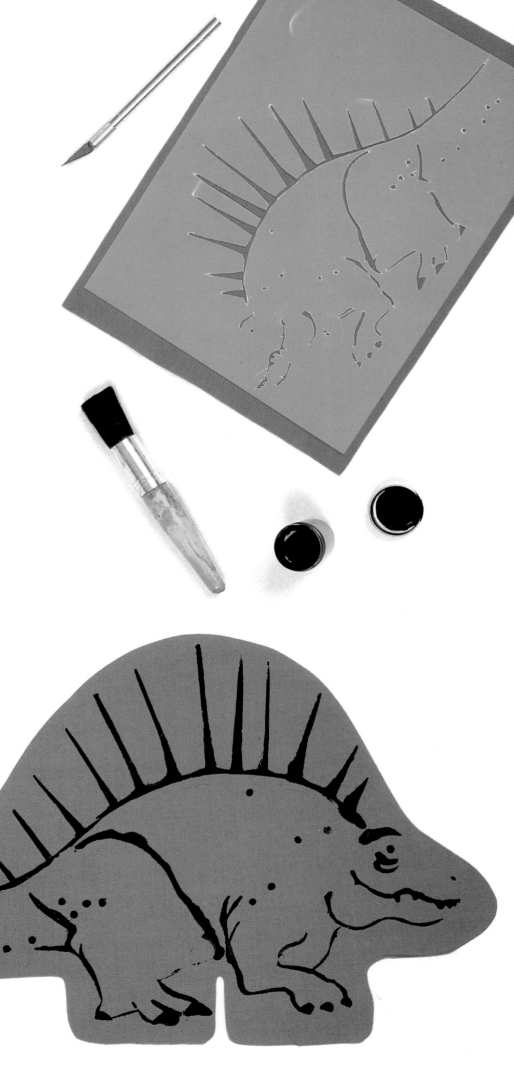

Stamps

Equipment

Large eraser

Craft knife or linoleum block cutting tools

Fabric paint

Brush

Fabric

Technique

1. Transfer design to eraser.

2. Using the craft knife, cut out the negative areas of the design. In other words, carve out the background areas you do not wish to print; the raised areas that you leave will form the design.

3. Brush paint onto the raised areas of the design.

4. Press stamp to fabric.

5. Allow paint to dry for about 12 hours.

6. Iron on reverse side of fabric to set paint.

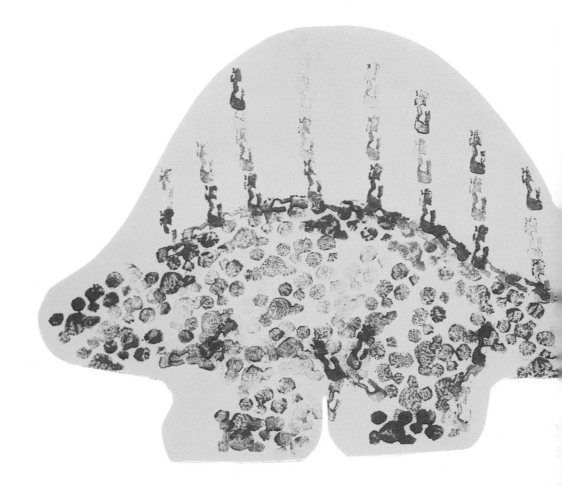

Note: In place of an eraser, you can use a medium-size potato. Simply cut it in half, carve out the background areas of your design on its cut surface, and proceed as directed above.

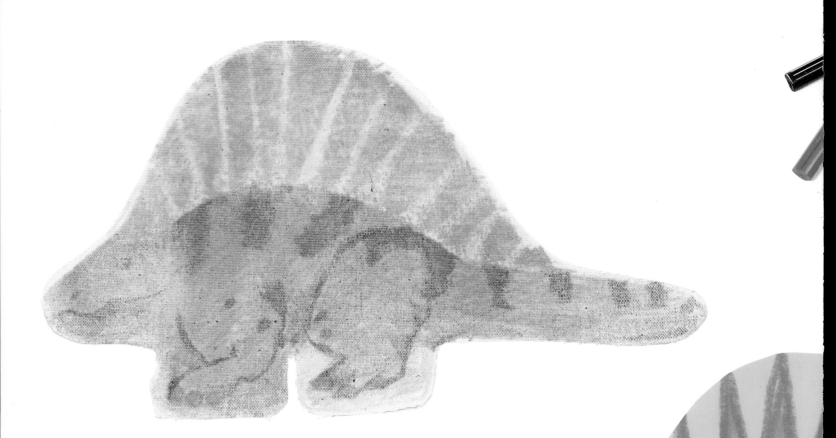

Fabric Crayons

Equipment

Transfer crayons

Tracing paper or regular white paper

Iron

Fabric (These crayons do best with synthetics but will work with a 60% polyester/40% cotton blend.)

Technique

1. Trace design onto tracing paper, or draw it on white paper. Remember that your design will be transferred onto the fabric in reverse.

2. Using firm pressure, color in your design. Brush away excess crayon specks.

3. Make an ironing pad by placing an old sheet over a soft pad of newspapers.

4. Lay fabric on top of pad, and iron to remove any wrinkles.

5. Place paper design face down on fabric, and pin the drawing in place at its corners.

6. Using a cotton setting on the iron, press the paper, ironing over the whole design. Don't allow the paper to move, or the design will blur.

7. Allow the paper to cool, then remove it carefully. (Design can be reused if color is reapplied.)

Fabric crayons, dye pastels, and fabric markers are wonderful materials. Fast, easy, and relatively inexpensive, they are perfect for children, who will begin enthusiastically to decorate their dinosaurs.

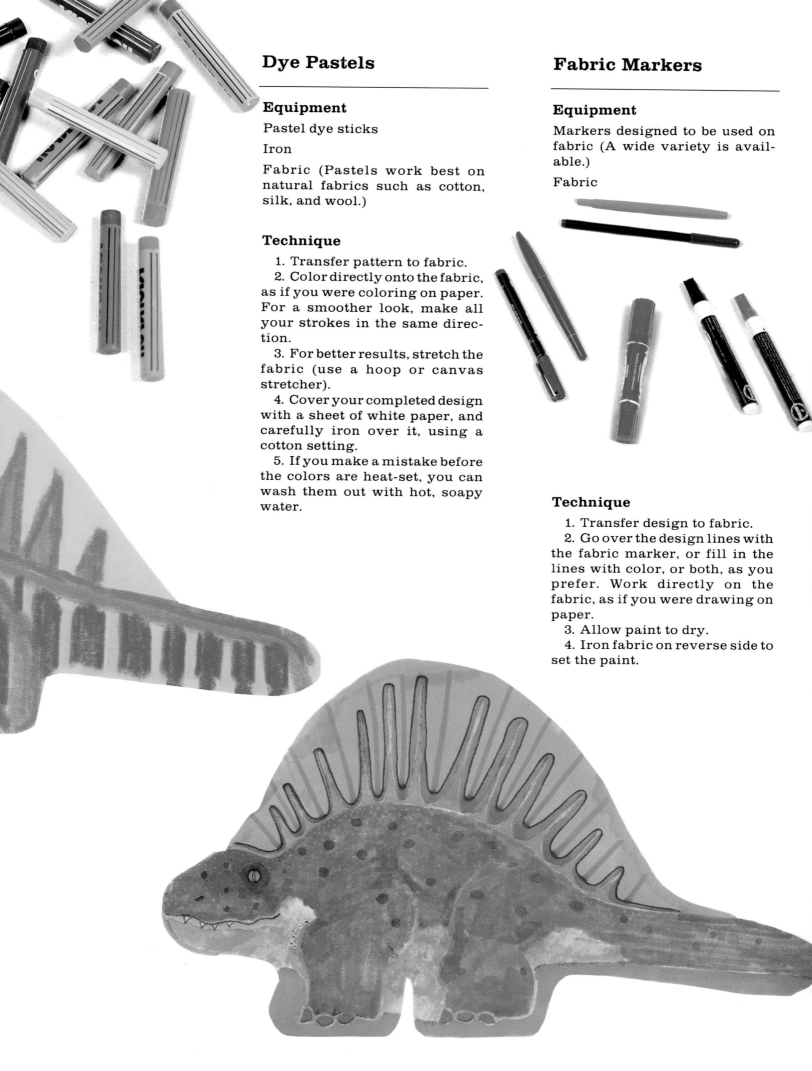

Dye Pastels

Equipment

Pastel dye sticks

Iron

Fabric (Pastels work best on natural fabrics such as cotton, silk, and wool.)

Technique

1. Transfer pattern to fabric.
2. Color directly onto the fabric, as if you were coloring on paper. For a smoother look, make all your strokes in the same direction.
3. For better results, stretch the fabric (use a hoop or canvas stretcher).
4. Cover your completed design with a sheet of white paper, and carefully iron over it, using a cotton setting.
5. If you make a mistake before the colors are heat-set, you can wash them out with hot, soapy water.

Fabric Markers

Equipment

Markers designed to be used on fabric (A wide variety is available.)

Fabric

Technique

1. Transfer design to fabric.
2. Go over the design lines with the fabric marker, or fill in the lines with color, or both, as you prefer. Work directly on the fabric, as if you were drawing on paper.
3. Allow paint to dry.
4. Iron fabric on reverse side to set the paint.

Silk Painting

Traditional silk paints require considerable practice and expertise to use properly. Their main drawback is that the inks have to be steamed in order to set. Fortunately, there are some new products on the market—Deka Silk and Peintex Silk—that do not require steaming. These easy-to-use paints can give excellent results even if you have never attempted any fabric painting before.

These instructions are specifically for the sled kite.

Equipment

Silk fabric

Felt-tip marker

Water-soluble fabric marking pens

Canvas-stretcher strips (for artists' canvas) or 1″ x 2″ (2.5 x 5 cm.) wood strips

Thumbtacks

Resist

Watercolor or foam brushes

Silk paints

Technique

1. Wash fabric to remove any sizing; dry and press it.
2. With a felt-tip marker, draw the enlarged kite pattern on a piece of paper.
3. Tape fabric over pattern. Since the China silk recommended for kites is transparent, you will be able to see the felt-tip marker lines through it.
4. Transferring the pattern to the fabric is the most difficult part of painting on silk; it requires lots of patience and a light touch to keep the fluid silk from shifting. And accurate pattern transfer is a must if your kite is to fly. I have found that if I spray the paper pattern with craft spray adhesive, the silk won't shift and I can achieve greater accuracy.

With a soft pencil, trace the cutting and stitching lines. With a water-soluble fabric pen (the kind that washes out of fabric), trace the design image that you will be painting.

5. Make a frame from the canvas stretcher strips (available at art supply and craft stores) or cut the 1″ x 2″ (2.5 x 5 cm.) strips of wood to the proper sizes and secure them at the corners to make a frame. Stretch the silk tightly on the frame, using lots of thumbtacks.

6. Apply resist to the design lines. Aptly named, "resist" is available wherever silk paints are sold. Silk paints flow across the fabric. Resist blocks the paint from flowing any farther, acting as a fence to keep the paint contained in specific areas.

Hold the bottle of resist vertically, with the tip firmly against the fabric, and squeeze gently while following the lines. Be sure that each shape is completely defined; even a small break can allow dye to escape.

As you apply the resist, the water-soluble marker will disappear, but your pencil-marked cutting lines will remain. Don't worry if some of the marker does not dissolve as the resist is applied; when you wash out the resist, the marker will also dissolve.

7. Allow resist to dry.

8. With a soft brush, gently apply paint to the middle of outlined areas. It will flow onto the silk until it meets the resist. Rather than using strong brush strokes, allow the fabric to absorb the dye from the brush.

9. Allow paint to dry for about 12 hours.

10. Press fabric on reverse side, using a dry iron.

11. Wash out resist in water.

Note: It is also possible to paint on silk without using resist. The paint will act like watercolor on wet paper—flowing across the fabric to mix freely. The Ichthyosaurus wind sock on page 91 illustrates this technique.

General Instructions for Needlework

The following methods of surface design all use needle and thread. The handwork has the advantage of being portable, while the machine needlework combines the elegance of color and texture with mechanized speed. Both are free of toxic fumes and other industrial hazards.

1. Wash, dry, and iron the fabric.
2. Sketch out the design you wish to use.
3. Transfer your design to the fabric, using tailor's chalk or a water-soluble fabric marker.
4. When stitching is completed, press on reverse side. Use a towel under right side of fabric to keep stitches from being flattened.

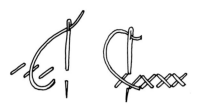

Cross Stitch

Stem Stitch

Embroidery

This ancient craft has been practiced by many cultures for hundreds of years. Variations include blackwork, crewelwork, tambour, punch needle embroidery, and counted-thread cross-stitch. Undoubtedly I've omitted at least one type, perhaps even your favorite. In this book I have described only a few of the hundreds of embroidery stitches that exist.

I learned to embroider when I was young, and this technique has become for me as natural as writing. It is a very relaxing process, which can build slowly and beautifully. Embroidery adds a richness and texture that are unique. Use a little or a lot—whatever you have the time for—and it will all add up to terrific.

Equipment

Threads: wool, cotton, rayon

Needles

Hoop

Fabric

Technique

1. Place fabric into embroidery hoop. The hoop keeps the fabric taut and helps to insure pucker-free stitches.
2. Thread needle and knot end of thread. Push needle from back to front of fabric. Using the illustrations as a guide, stitch your design onto the fabric.

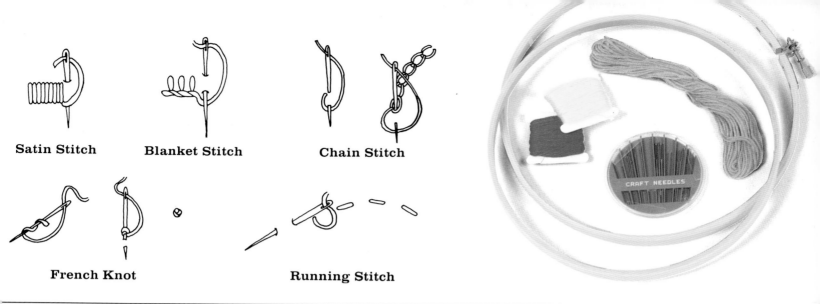

Satin Stitch

Blanket Stitch

Chain Stitch

French Knot

Running Stitch

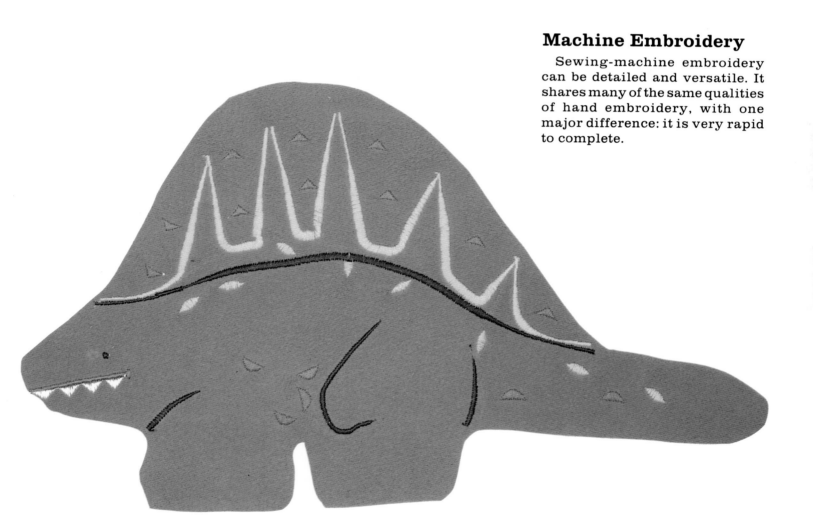

Machine Embroidery

Sewing-machine embroidery can be detailed and versatile. It shares many of the same qualities of hand embroidery, with one major difference: it is very rapid to complete.

Equipment

Sewing machine with decorative stitches

Thread

Fabric

Technique

Read your sewing machine manual for complete directions on using decorative stitches. In general, you'll proceed as follows:

1. Back the fabric with a sheet of tracing paper so that the stitches do not pucker the fabric. Using a regular foot, sew the embroidery. After the embroidery is complete, remove the paper.

2. In free-motion embroidery, the foot is removed and the fabric is placed in a hoop and manipulated in a design that can be loose and improvisational. You might want to combine hand and machine embroidery on the same dinosaur.

Quilting

This book contains no quilting in its traditional sense—no bed covers or garments to keep you warm. Rather, quilting serves as a decorative surface design or as a means to add structural stability to various parts of the dinosaurs.

Trapunto Quilting

Equipment

Fabric

Thread

Polyester fiberfill

Technique

1. Baste two layers of fabric wrong sides together. One layer will be the skin of your dinosaur; the other will act as a lining.

2. With water-soluble pen, outline the area you want to quilt.

3. Machine or hand stitch along marked design lines.

4. Cut slit in back of piece of fabric that forms the inside lining.

5. Insert fiberfill stuffing through cut opening.

6. Slipstitch over the slits to close.

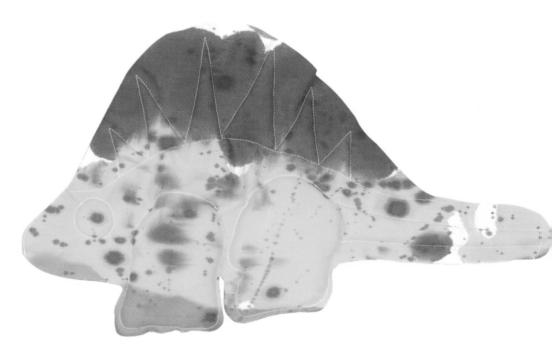

Machine Quilting

Equipment

Fabric

Polyester fiberfill batting

Thread

Technique

1. Transfer quilting design to fabric.

2. Make a sandwich of fabric, polyester fiberfill batting, and lining fabric.

3. Set the sewing machine to a medium-large stitch.

4. Stitch through fabric, fiberfill, and lining, following markings on fabric.

Appliqué

In appliqué a motif cut from one piece of fabric is placed on another and, frequently, stitched in place around the edges. The stitching can be decorative handwork or done by machine. Match the weight and fiber content of the appliqué fabrics to those of the background material.

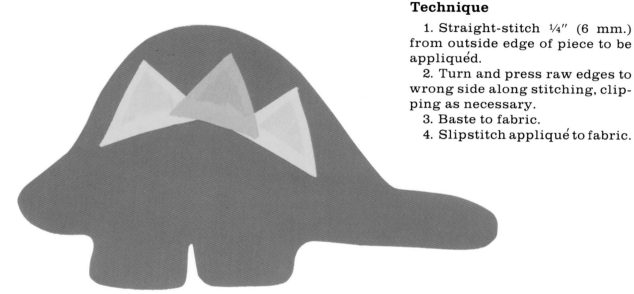

Hand-stitched Appliqué

Equipment

Fabric

Thread

Technique

1. Straight-stitch ¼″ (6 mm.) from outside edge of piece to be appliquéd.
2. Turn and press raw edges to wrong side along stitching, clipping as necessary.
3. Baste to fabric.
4. Slipstitch appliqué to fabric.

Fusible Web Appliqué

Equipment

Fusible web

Fabric

Thread

Technique

1. Cut appliqué and fusible web from same pattern.

2. With fusible web between appliqué and fabric, pin appliqué in position on fabric.
3. Iron appliqué in position. You can either leave the appliqué as it is or secure it in place, choosing from two methods.
4. Slick dimensional paint can dress up a fusible-web appliqué.

Just apply squeeze bottle paint along raw edges of appliqué to seal the edges and prevent fraying. Allow paint to dry 12 hours, and iron on reverse side to set the paint.
5. Or sew appliqué to fabric with your sewing machine: outline appliqué with a satin stitch.

Eyes

It has been said that the eyes are the windows of the soul. Certainly they are important elements in giving each of the dinosaurs its distinctive personality.

Each pattern contains a suggested eye treatment. However, feel free to use alternate methods on any of the projects.

Safety Eyes

These are good choices for toys that are destined for small children. Designed to make it difficult for children to pull them off and possibly swallow or choke on them, safety eyes come attached to a stem. An accompanying washer is secured to the stem before the toy is stuffed. Not only are these eyes difficult for children to remove, but they are also difficult for adults to remove, so be sure you have them placed correctly before you secure the washer.

Equipment

Safety eyes (available in craft supply stores, or see "Mail-Order Sources," page 127)

Technique

1. Mark fabric where you want to install the eye.
2. With scissors, cut a small slit in fabric at the mark.
3. Insert safety eye stem through slit, leaving eye on right side of fabric.
4. Place washer over end of stem, and squeeze tightly in place.

Buttons

Widely available in many colors, shapes, and sizes, buttons make excellent eyes.

Technique

1. Mark fabric where you want to locate the eye.
2. Thread needle with a strong thread such as carpet thread or buttonhole thread. Dental floss also makes a good strong thread for attaching eyes.
3. Sew through shank or holes of button several times. Knot thread securely on wrong side of fabric.

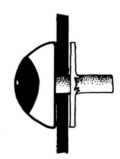

Embroidery

Embroidered eyes are also safe for small children. You can be more elaborate and provide lots of color and detail with your embroidery thread. See "Embroidery," page 28, for a discussion of technique.

Felt

Not only are felt eyes safe for small children, but they provide a fast way of applying an eye. They can be stitched or glued in place.

Technique

1. Cut eyes from felt.
2. Position felt on fabric.
3. Glue or slipstitch eye in place on fabric.

Squeakers, Growlers, and Music Boxes

Some of the devices that will bring audio to your dinosaurs are hard to find in many areas. Fortunately, they are available from mail-order companies that specialize in accessories for bears and dolls (see "Mail-Order Sources, page 127). Squeakers can be dropped into the cavities created for them in various patterns later in the book. To install a growler or music box, proceed as follows:

Technique

1. Cut a piece of fabric wide enough to go around the box and long enough to cover the ends.
2. Stitch a fabric bag with one end open.
3. Insert music device into bag.
4. Stitch fabric bag closed.
5. Stitch bag securely to seams, as directed on individual patterns.

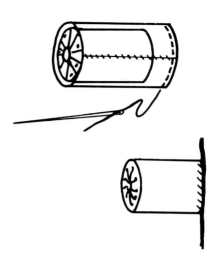

Joints

Joining the arms and legs to the body is a critical step in toy making. These joints are generally the weakest part of the doll, and, after all, an arm or leg is the handle by which the doll is transported throughout its life.

Whenever possible, I have tried to design the legs and arms as a unit to be attached to the body by machine sewing. This is a very secure method and has the additional advantage of allowing the limbs to be stuffed through the body cavity, thus leaving only one hand-closed opening. Sometimes the legs are actually cut with the body.

For a dinosaur that needs more freedom of movement, a movable plastic joint is the perfect choice. Plastic joints are attached to the toy after the limbs are pieced together and the body is stitched up but before they are stuffed.

1. Cut a small slit on the inside of the limb—let's say, the arm—at the marking on the pattern.
2. Insert the plastic joint into the arm, with the stem protruding.
3. Cut a small slit on the body where marked. Push the stem through the body to the wrong side.
4. Place the washer on the stem, and secure with the locking washer. Be sure to push the locking washer on tightly.

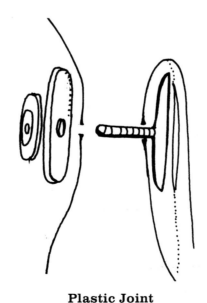

Plastic Joint

A ribbon joint can also let a dinosaur move around, especially if it's a small toy. This kind of joint is constructed after the limbs and body are stuffed.

1. Thread a long, large-eye tapestry needle with 24" (60 cm.) of ⅛" (3 mm.) ribbon.
2. Push the needle through an arm at the pattern marking. Proceed through the body at its markings, and continue through the remaining arm.
3. Go back through arm-body-arm.
4. Holding both ends of the ribbon, pull it snug and knot it at both ends, finishing off with a decorative bow on each arm.

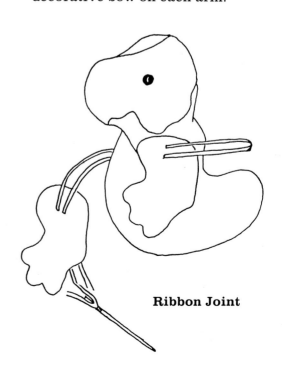

Ribbon Joint

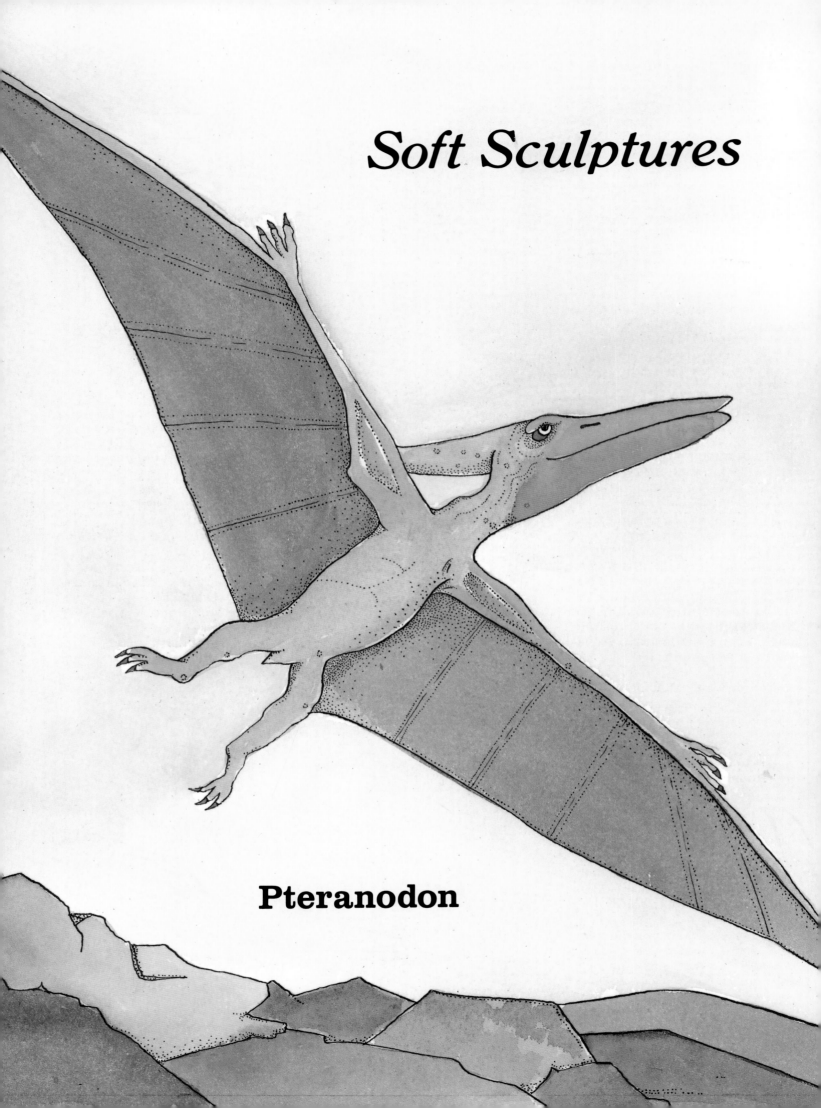

Soft Sculptures

Pteranodon

Pteranodon

Pteranodon (ter-AN-o-don) lived at the height of the Age of Dinosaurs, the late Cretaceous period. Since dinosaurs lived only on land, many prehistoric animals cannot be considered dinosaurs. In the air were the pterosaurs, a separate group of gliding and flying reptiles. Pteranodon was one of the largest of these. Equipped with leathery wings, a powerful neck, and pelican-like jaws, Pteranodons soared across the skies for millions of years, until their extinction about 60 million years ago.

This pattern will sew a realistic model with a 50″ (125 cm.) wingspan.

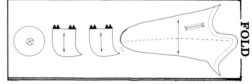

FABRIC REQUIREMENTS

A woven, lightweight to medium weight broadcloth. Because this is a flying reptile, I like to sew Pteranodon from sky colors.

45″ (112 cm.) fabric
Main color:
    1⅜ yds. (135 cm.)
Beak, eyeball, claws:
    ¼ yd. (23 cm.)
Nostril (outside):
    2″ x 3″ (5 x 7.5 cm.)
Nostril (inside):
    2″ by 3″ (5 x 7.5 cm.)
¼ yd. (23 cm.) iron-on interfacing

NOTIONS

Two 19 mm. safety eyes.
1 lb. (½ kg.) polyester fiberfill stuffing
½ yd. (45 cm.) polyester fiberfill batting
Matching thread

PATTERN PIECES

1. BEAK
2. BODY
3. NOSTRIL
4. EYE SOCKET
5. EYE
6. ARM
7. LEG
8. WING
9. CLAW

Pteranodon Layout

SEAM ALLOWANCE IS ¼″ (6 mm.)

FOLD

Contrasting Color

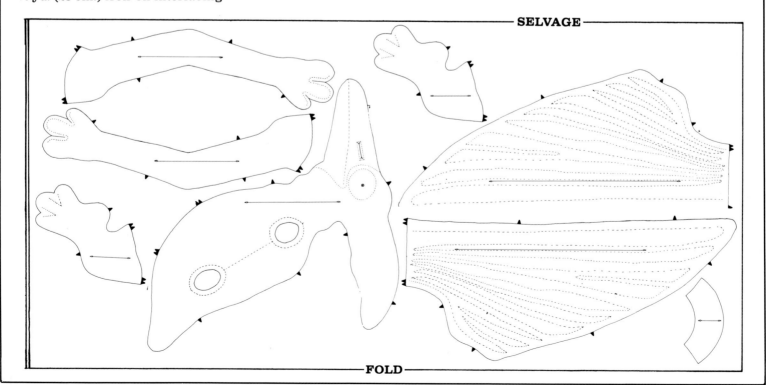

SELVAGE

FOLD

1.

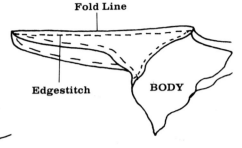

- Right sides together, matching notches, place interfacing (smooth side is right side) and beak together; pin.
- Stitch beak to interfacing as shown.
- Trim and clip seam.
- Turn right side out and iron interfacing to wrong side of fabric. This will result in a smooth finished edge.

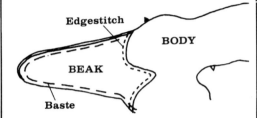

- Place beak right side up on right side of body, matching finished edge of beak to stitching line. Pin.
- Edgestitch along finished edge.
- Baste remaining loose edges of beak to body.
- Repeat for remaining beak.

2.

- Fold beak wrong sides together along fold line.
- Press.
- Edgestitch ⅛" (3 mm.) from fold line.
- Press mouth fold down, away from top of head.
- Repeat for mouth on other side of body.

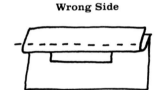

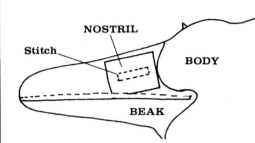

- Right sides together, center nostril over markings on body. Baste.
- Using small, tight stitches, stitch along stitching line, pivoting at corners, through rectangle and body, following nostril markings.

3.

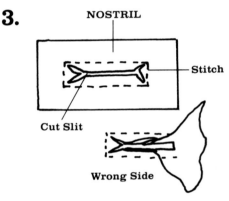

- Cut a slit between stitching, through both layers of fabric.
- Push nostril material through the opening, to the wrong side of body.

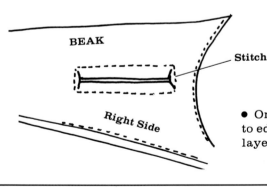

- Fold both long sides of the rectangle to form the "lips" of the nostril.
- Crease sharply along stitching at the corners to make them clean cut. Each of the lips fills ½ the open space of opening. Press.
- Center a contrast-color nostril under opening, right side of contrast color to wrong side of body. Baste.

- On right side of fabric, stitch close to edge of opening through all fabric layers.

4.

- Staystitch top of eye socket.

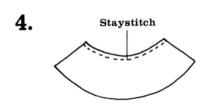

- Fold eye socket in half, right sides facing; stitch side seam. Press seam open.

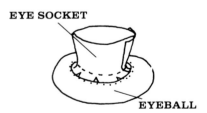

- Clip staystitched edge of eye socket.
- Right sides together, match cut edge of eye socket to dotted line on eye. Pin and baste pieces together.
- Stitch eye to eye socket.
- Trim seam.
- Turn eye assembly right side out.

5.

- Turn under ¼" (6 mm.) on remaining raw edge on eye socket. Pin to body as marked. Baste. Edgestitch in place. Note: Position of side seam in eye socket is seam facing down when joining to body.
- Repeat for remaining eye and eye socket.

- Apply safety eyes through eye and body.

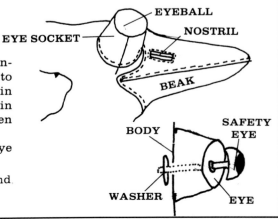

36

6.

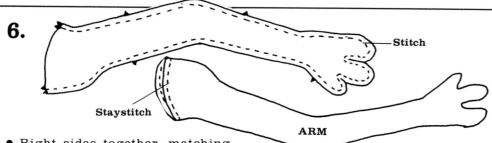

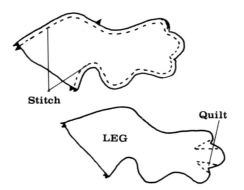

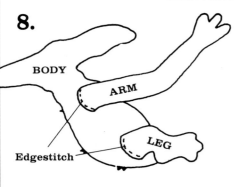

- Right sides together, matching notches, pin two arm pieces together.
- Stitch from double notch to double notch; leave opening between double notches.
- Clip curves and trim around fingers.
- Turn arm right side out.
- Press.
- Staystitch arm socket.
- Repeat for remaining arm pieces.

- Right sides together, matching notches, pin two leg pieces together.
- Stitch from double notch to double notch; leave opening between double notches.
- Clip curves.
- Turn leg right side out. Press.

- Machine quilt along stitching line between toes.
- Staystitch leg socket.
- Repeat for remaining leg pieces.

7.

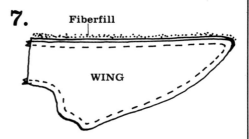

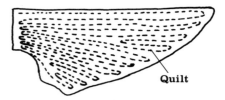

- Right sides together, matching notches, pin two wing pieces together. Place the two wing pieces on top of wing fiberfill batting. Pin the fabric pieces and fiberfill batting together.
- Stitch from double notch to double notch; leave opening between double notches.
- Clip curves and trim seams.

- Turn through opening between wing pieces.
- Press. Turn under seam allowance on open end. Baste closed.
- Machine quilt following stitching lines.
- Repeat for remaining wing.

8.

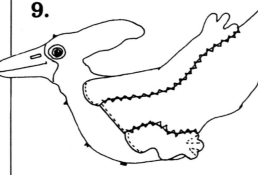

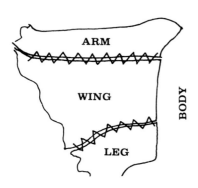

- Turn under seam allowance on arm.
- Pin arm to markings on body, matching seams to circles. Baste.
- Edgestitch arm to body.
- Repeat for remaining arm.
- Repeat for legs.

- Starting at arm/body joint, butt long straight edge of wing next to arm seam. Use a small zigzag stitch to join pieces together.
- Butt upper edge of leg to lower edge of wing. Use a small zigzag stitch to join pieces together.

9.

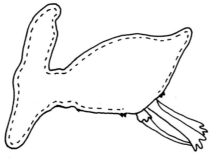

- To join wing to body, pin wing edge to line between arm and leg. Edgestitch wing to body.
- Repeat for remaining side of body.

- Right sides together, matching notches, pin the two body pieces together. Arrange the arm-wing-leg assemblies to exit between the double notches. Take care not to catch arm-wing-leg in seam.
- Stitch from double notch to double notch; leave opening between double notches.
- Clip curves.
- Turn Pteranodon right side out through opening.

10.

- Stuff fingers and arms.
- Stuff toes and legs.
- Stuff beak, crest, and the rest of the head.
- Stuff neck and body.
- Baste opening closed.
- Slipstitch opening closed.

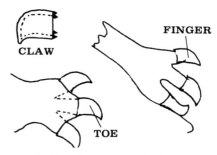

- Right sides together, pin two claw pieces together.
- Stitch from double notch to double notch.
- Clip, and turn right side out.
- Lightly stuff claw. Turn under seam allowance on raw edge.
- Pin a claw to a fingertip.
- Hand-stitch claw to fingertip, using a slipstitch.
- Repeat for all fingers.
- Repeat for all toes.

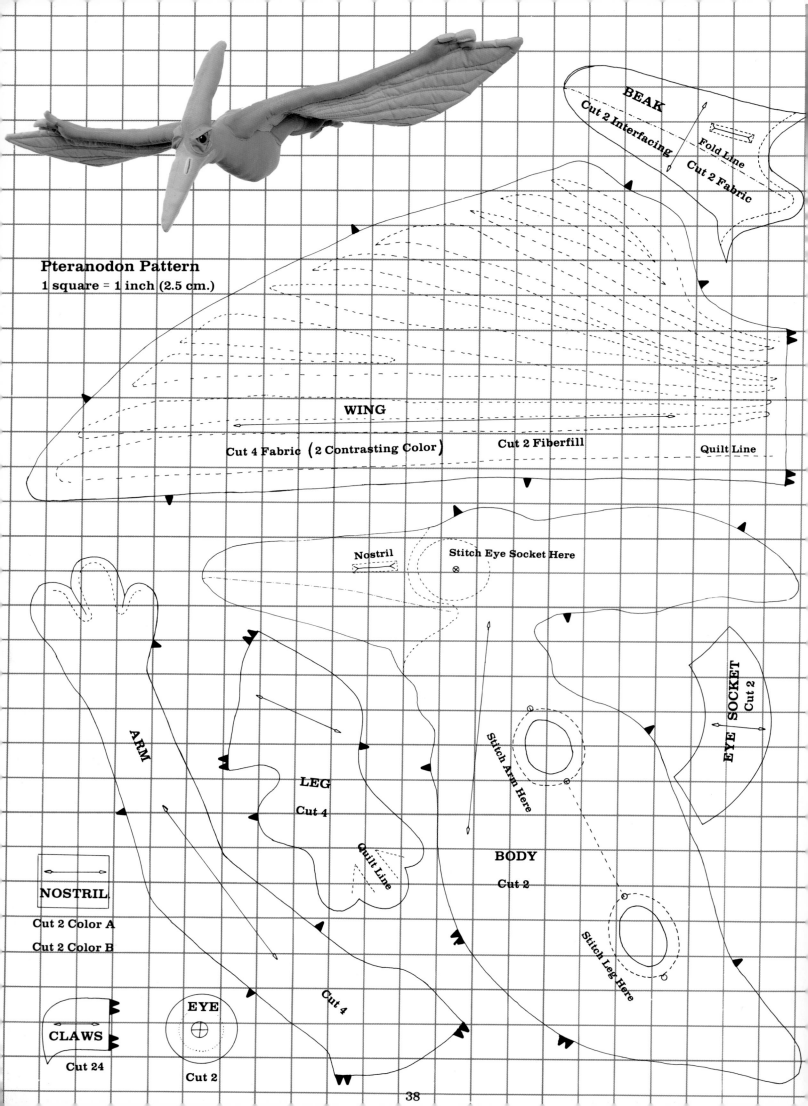

Pteranodon Pattern
1 square = 1 inch (2.5 cm.)

BEAK
Cut 2 Interfacing
Cut 2 Fabric
Fold Line

WING
Cut 4 Fabric (2 Contrasting Color)   Cut 2 Fiberfill   Quilt Line

Nostril   Stitch Eye Socket Here

EYE SOCKET
Cut 2

ARM

LEG
Cut 4

Stitch Arm Here

Quilt Line

BODY
Cut 2

NOSTRIL
Cut 2 Color A
Cut 2 Color B

Stitch Leg Here

Cut 4

CLAWS
Cut 24

EYE
Cut 2

Apatosaurus

Apatosaurus Herd

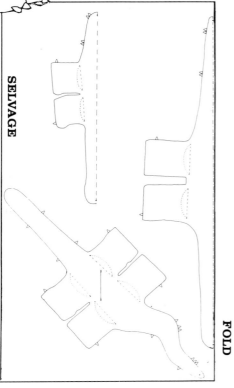

Apatosaurus (a-PAT-o-SORE-us). This giant, plant-eating dinosaur is also known by the name Brontosaurus—"thunder lizard"—but according to the rules for scientific naming, the first name given to its remains, Apatosaurus, is more officially correct. The name Apatosaurus means "deceptive reptile." Apatosaurus fossils have been found in the United States. This vegetarian was huge: 65 feet (20 meters) long and 33 tons (30 metric tons). Apatosaurus could have used its heavy tail as a great whiplash to deter attackers.

This pattern will sew three sizes of Apatosaurus: small (12½″, or 31 cm.); medium (19″, or 46 cm.); and large (21″, or 53 cm.). Make a group of them and have your own herd of Apatosaurus.

Apatosaurus Herd Layout

Cut large and medium gusset pieces; then refold fabric and cut small gusset.

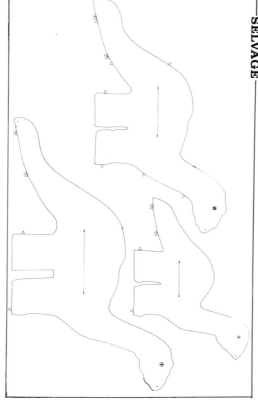

FABRIC REQUIREMENTS

Apatosaurus's fabric resulted from a browsing session at the "sale" table at my local fabric store. I was looking for three colors of fabric to sew my herd from, and a delightful dotted print and harmonizing solids were sitting there waiting for me—and at a bargain price. I added some fabric paint to draw the hoofs and shadows, and voila—a herd of Apatosaurus!

45″ (112 cm.) fabric
(Fabric amounts are for all three Apatosaurus.)
Body color:
    1 yd. (90 cm.)
Gusset color:
    1 yd. (90 cm.)

NOTIONS

Six 9 mm. ball-type safety eyes
2 lbs. (1 kg.) polyester fiberfill
    stuffing
Matching thread

PATTERN PIECES

1. BODY
2. GUSSET

SEAM ALLOWANCE IS ¼″ (6 mm.)

Apatosaurus Herd Assembly

1.

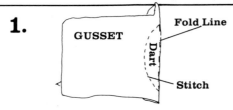

- To sew darts in gusset, fold on dot-dashed line, right sides together.
- Pin and stitch along dashed line.

2.

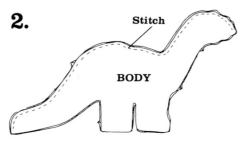

- Right sides together, matching notches, pin body pieces together. Stitch from circle to circle.

3.

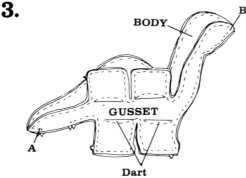

- Right sides together, matching notches, pin gusset to the right side of the body. Baste. Stitch from A to B. Leave opening between double notches.

- Repeat for gusset to left side of body. Do not leave opening between double notches.

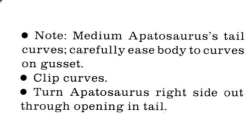

- Note: Medium Apatosaurus's tail curves; carefully ease body to curves on gusset.
- Clip curves.
- Turn Apatosaurus right side out through opening in tail.

4.

- Apply eyes.
- Stuff head and neck.
- Stuff legs.
- Stuff body.
- Stuff tail.
- Hand-stitch opening in tail closed.

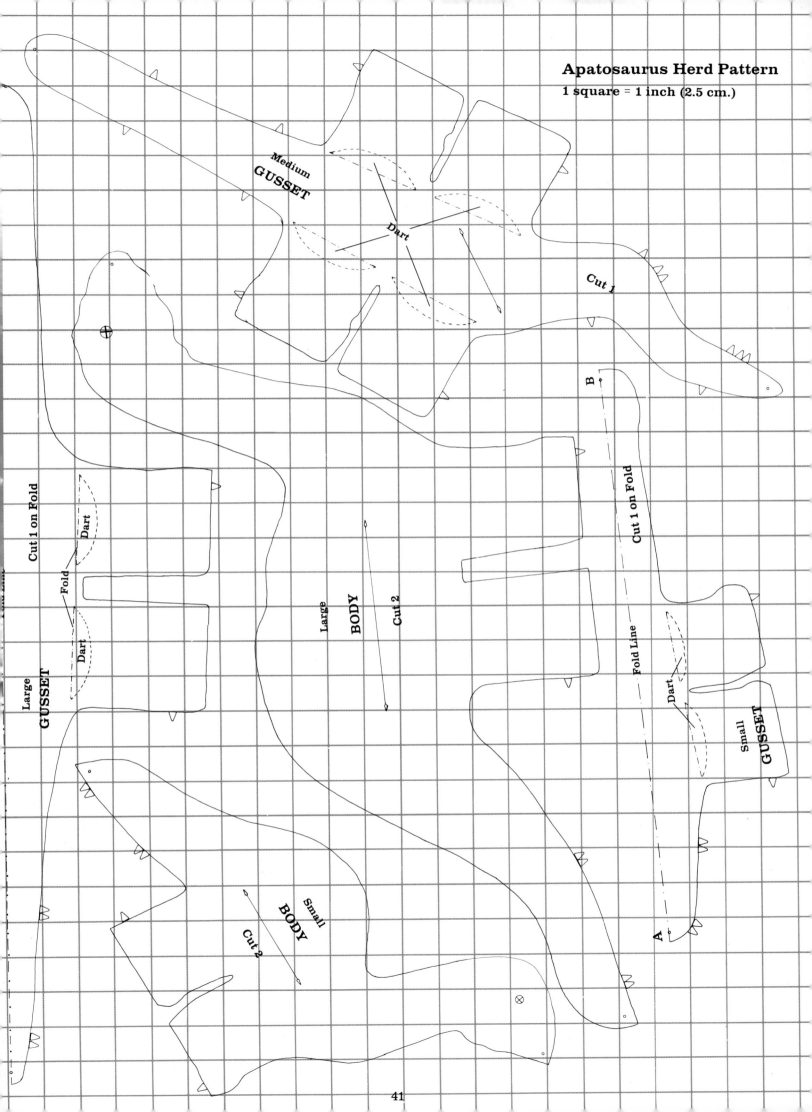

Apatosaurus Herd Pattern
1 square = 1 inch (2.5 cm.)

Medium
GUSSET

Dart

Cut 1

B

Cut 1 on Fold

Cut 1 on Fold

Dart
Fold
Dart

Large
GUSSET

Large
BODY
Cut 2

Fold Line

Dart

Small
GUSSET

Small
BODY
Cut 2

A

41

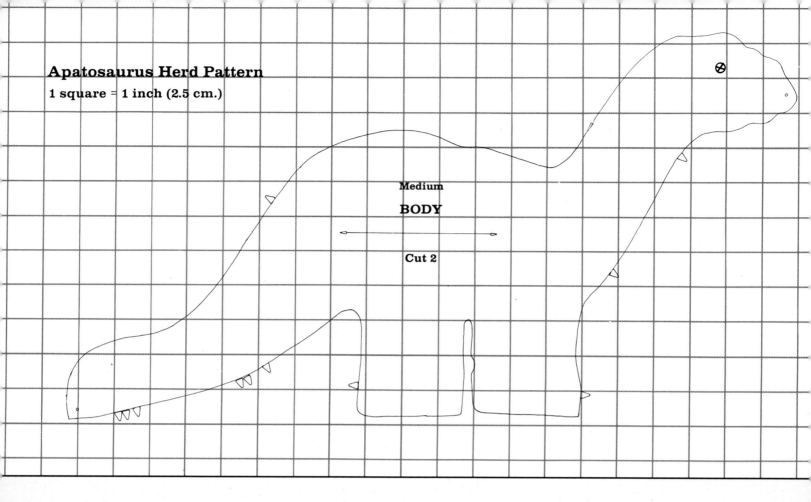

Apatosaurus Herd Pattern
1 square = 1 inch (2.5 cm.)

Medium

BODY

Cut 2

Triceratops

Triceratops

Triceratops (try-SER-a-tops) was a North American dinosaur who roamed the western plains millions of years ago. "Three-horned face" was named for its horns: one on its nose and two long ones above its eyes. At 30 feet (nine meters) long and about 12 tons (11 metric tons), this big-horned plant eater was nearly twice as large as an African elephant, the largest land animal of today.

This pattern will sew a 26" (65 cm.) long realistic model of this giant reptile.

Triceratops Layout

FABRIC REQUIREMENTS

Triceratops was a vegetarian, so I like to sew him in green, a color that just seems to suit him.

45" (112 cm.) fabric
Main color:
    1¼ yds. (113 cm.)
Contrast color A (eye/nose):
    4" x 4" (10 by 10 cm.)
Contrast color B (eye/nose):
    4" x 4" (10 by 10 cm.)
Horn color:
    ¼ yd. (23 cm.)
¼ yd. (23 cm.) iron-on interfacing

NOTIONS

Scraps of felt for eyes
2 lbs. (1 kg.) polyester fiberfill
    stuffing
¼ yd. (23 cm.) polyester fiberfill
    batting.
Matching thread
Contrasting thread

SEAM ALLOWANCE IS ¼" (6 mm.)

PATTERN PIECES

1. BODY
2. FRONT LEGS
3. FRONT FEET
4. BACK LEGS
5. BACK FEET
6. COWL
7. EYELID
8. HORNS
9. NOSE HORN
10. NECK GUIDE
11. EYE/NOSE GUIDE

SELVAGE

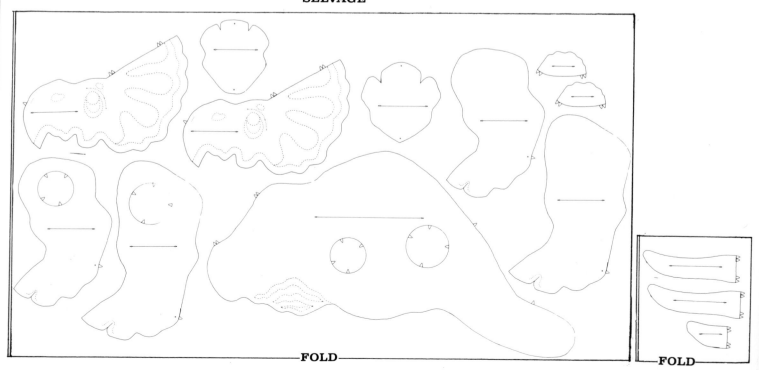

FOLD

FOLD

1.

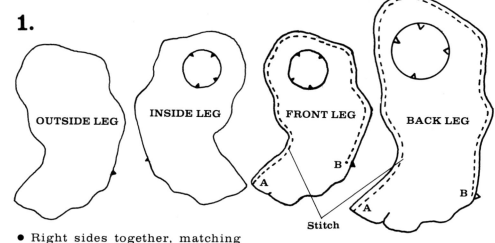

OUTSIDE LEG   INSIDE LEG   FRONT LEG   BACK LEG

Stitch

- Right sides together, matching notches, pin inside front leg and outside front leg together.
- Stitch around front leg from A to B.
- Repeat for remaining front leg pieces.
- Repeat for back leg pieces.

2.

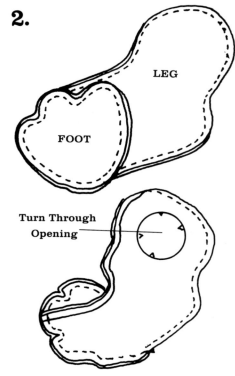

LEG

FOOT

Turn Through Opening

- Right sides together, matching outside edges, pin front foot to bottom of front leg.
- Stitch foot to leg; use stitching line as marked on pattern for area between toes.
- Clip curves on leg and foot.

- Turn leg/foot right side out through opening on inside leg.
- Repeat for remaining front leg and front foot.
- Repeat for back legs and back feet.

3.

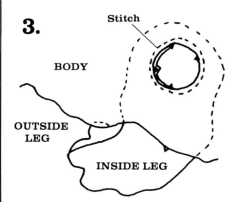

Stitch

BODY

OUTSIDE LEG

INSIDE LEG

- Right sides together, matching notches, pin front leg opening on body to opening on inside of front leg.
- Stitch front leg to body.
- Repeat for remaining front leg.
- Repeat for back legs.

4.

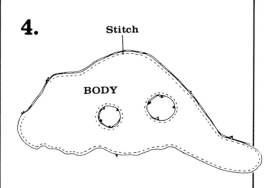

Stitch

BODY

- Right sides together, matching notches, pin the two body pieces together. Take care to keep legs from getting caught in seam.
- Stitch; leave opening between double notches.
- Clip curves.
- Turn body right side out.

5.

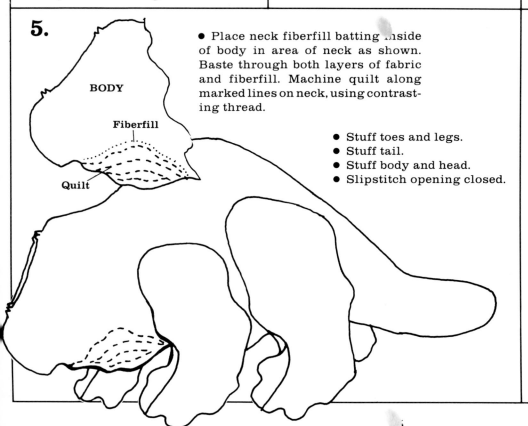

BODY

Fiberfill

Quilt

- Place neck fiberfill batting inside of body in area of neck as shown. Baste through both layers of fabric and fiberfill. Machine quilt along marked lines on neck, using contrasting thread.

- Stuff toes and legs.
- Stuff tail.
- Stuff body and head.
- Slipstitch opening closed.

6.

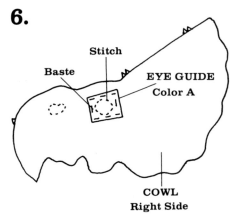

Stitch

Baste

EYE GUIDE
Color A

COWL
Right Side

- Right sides together, center eye/nose guide (color A) over marked eye on right side of cowl. Baste as shown.
- Using small, tight stitches, stitch along eye stitching line marked on cowl..
- Repeat for remaining eye guide to left side of cowl.
- Repeat for nose guide to right and left sides of cowl.

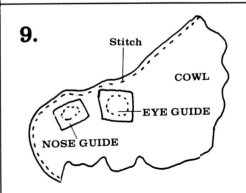

7.

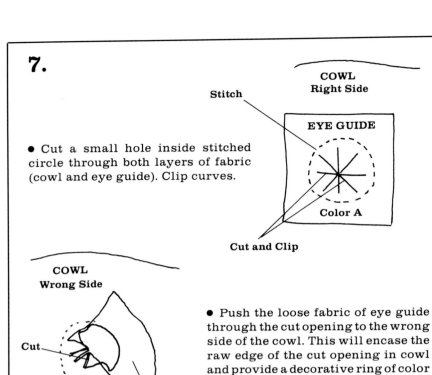

● Cut a small hole inside stitched circle through both layers of fabric (cowl and eye guide). Clip curves.

● Push the loose fabric of eye guide through the cut opening to the wrong side of the cowl. This will encase the raw edge of the cut opening in cowl and provide a decorative ring of color at the eye.

● Press.

Triceratops Assembly

8.

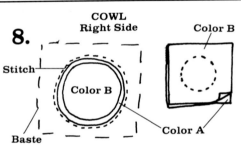

● Center eye guide (color B) on wrong side of cowl under eye opening that was formed with eye color A. Right side of eye guide (color B) and cowl should be facing up. Baste.

● On right side of fabric, stitch close to edge of opening (color A) through all three fabric layers.

● Repeat for eye guides and left side of cowl.

● Repeat for nose guides and right and left sides of cowl.

9.

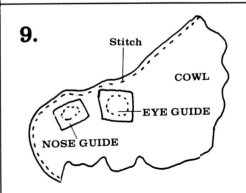

● Right sides together, matching notches, stitch cowl center seam together.

10.

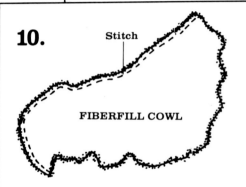

● Matching notches, sew center seam of fiberfill batting cowl together.

11.

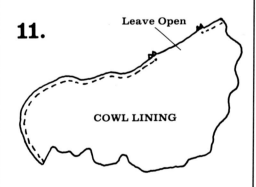

● Following manufacturer's directions, apply iron-on-interfacing to cowl lining.

● Right sides together, matching notches, pin cowl lining together.

● Stitch center seam; leave open between double notches.

12.

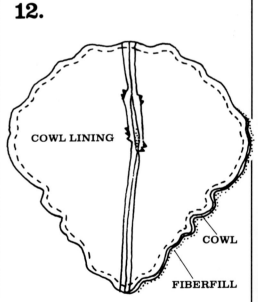

● Place cowl and cowl lining right sides together, notches matching. Place fiberfill batting cowl on top of cowl, matching outside edges. Make sure the cowl lining is on top of sandwich. Pin all three pieces together.

● Stitch around outside of cowl sandwich.

● Clip curves and trim seams.

● Turn between fabric pieces through opening in cowl lining.

● Press, turning under seam allowance on cowl lining. Hand-stitch closed.

46

13.

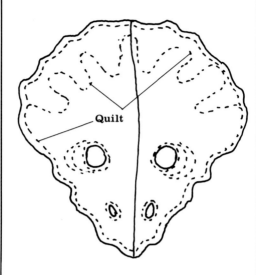

Quilt

- With contrasting thread, machine-quilt cowl, following stitching lines marked on pattern.

- Apply eyes: cut two ¼″ (6 mm.) circles from felt, and stitch or glue in place.

14.

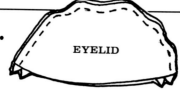

EYELID

- Apply iron-on interfacing to wrong side of eyelid.
- Right sides together, pin two eyelid pieces together.
- Stitch as shown.
- Turn and press.
- Turn under ¼″ (6 mm.) seam allow-ance on unfinished edge. Pin and baste along markings on cowl. Stitch.

15.

NOSE HORN

HORN

- Right sides together, pin two horn pieces together.
- Stitch as shown.
- Clip and turn right side out.
- Repeat for remaining horns.

16.

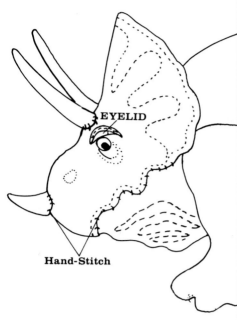

EYELID

Hand-Stitch

- Stuff horns. Turn under seam allowance on raw edge.
- Pin horns in place on cowl.
- Slipstitch horn to cowl.
- Repeat for remaining horns.
- Slipstitch cowl in place on body.

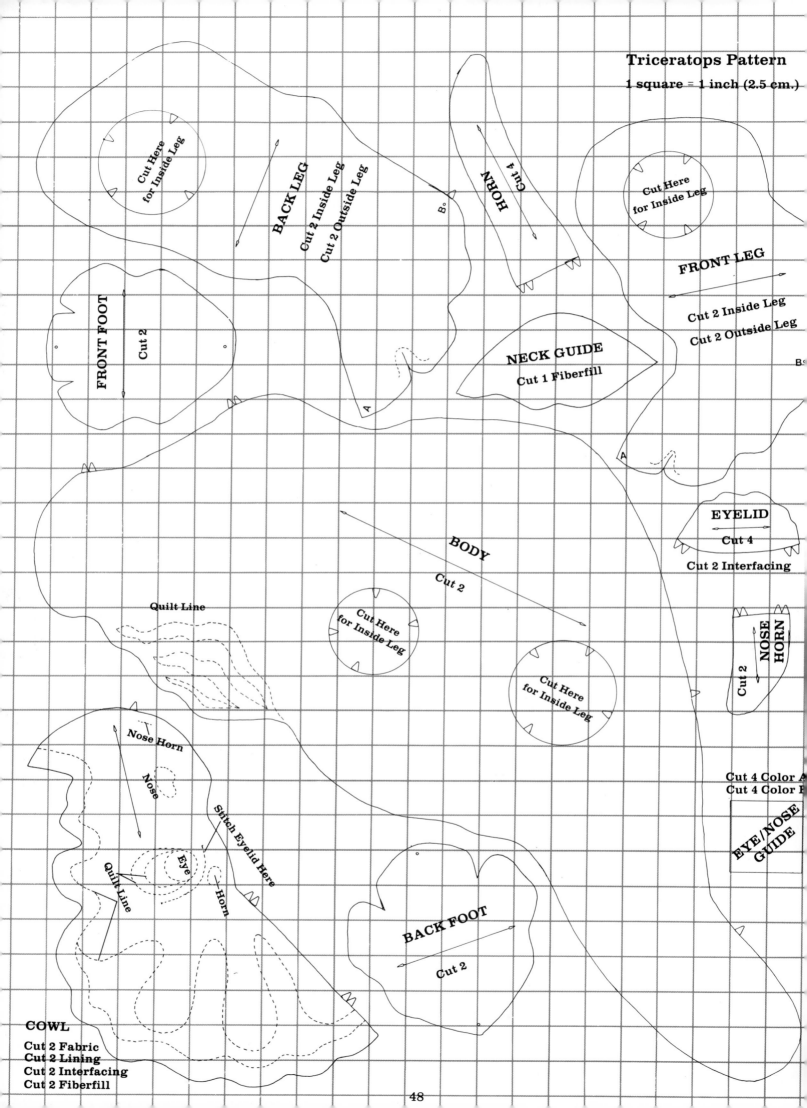

Triceratops Pattern

1 square = 1 inch (2.5 cm.)

Cut Here for Inside Leg

BACK LEG
Cut 2 Inside Leg
Cut 2 Outside Leg

HORN
Cut 4
B°

Cut Here for Inside Leg

FRONT LEG
Cut 2 Inside Leg
Cut 2 Outside Leg
B°

FRONT FOOT
Cut 2

NECK GUIDE
Cut 1 Fiberfill

A
A

EYELID
Cut 4
Cut 2 Interfacing

BODY
Cut 2

Quilt Line

Cut Here for Inside Leg

Cut Here for Inside Leg

NOSE HORN
Cut 2

Cut 4 Color A
Cut 4 Color B

Nose Horn

Nose

Stitch Eyelid Here

Quilt Line

Eye

Horn

EYE/NOSE GUIDE

BACK FOOT
Cut 2

COWL
Cut 2 Fabric
Cut 2 Lining
Cut 2 Interfacing
Cut 2 Fiberfill

Stegosaurus

Stegosaurus

Stegosaurus (steg-o-SORE-us) was a North American, plant-eating reptile who weighed four tons and was 30 feet (nine meters) long. He lived during the Jurassic period. Stegosaurus is called the "plated reptile" because its back was armed with great vertical plates. It had a tiny brain the size of a walnut.

This pattern will sew a 25" (63 cm.) long soft sculpture of Stegosaurus.

Stegosaurus Layout

FABRIC REQUIREMENTS

Stegosaurus was sewn of a medium weight broadcloth. Machine embroidery was used to highlight details on the plates and body, and dimensional paint was used to apply appliqués.

45" (112 cm.) fabric

Main color:
  1 yd. (90 cm.)
Contrast plates and spikes:
  1 yd. (90 cm.)

NOTIONS

Two 9mm. black ball-type safety eyes
2 lb. (1 kg.) fiberfill stuffing
½ yd. (45 cm.) polyester fiberfill batting
1 yd. (90 cm.) heavyweight iron-on interfacing
Matching thread
Contrasting thread

PATTERN PIECES

1. BODY
2. GUSSET
3. FRONT FEET
4. INSIDE BACK LEG
5. OUTSIDE BACK LEG
6. BACK FEET
7. PLATE A
8. PLATE B
9. PLATE C
10. PLATE D
11. PLATE E
12. SPIKE

SEAM ALLOWANCE IS ¼" (6 mm.)

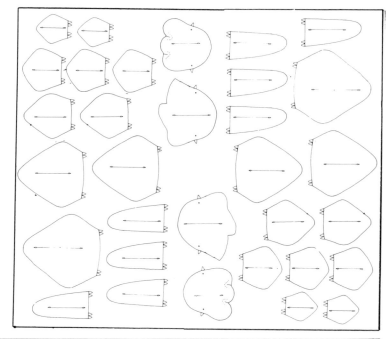

SELVAGE

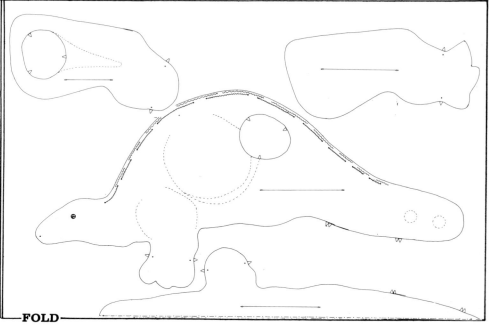

FOLD

1.

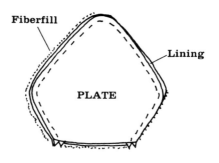

Fiberfill

Lining

PLATE

- Following manufacturer's instructions, apply iron-on interfacing to wrong side of plates.
- Right sides together, matching notches, pin two plates together. Place the matched plates on top of a matching piece of fiberfill. Pin fabric-fiberfill sandwich together.
- Stitch from double notch to double notch, as shown.
- Clip and trim seam.
- Turn between fabric pieces. Press.
- Machine quilt plate as shown, using contrasting thread.
- Repeat for all remaining plates.

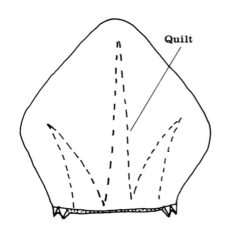

Quilt

2.

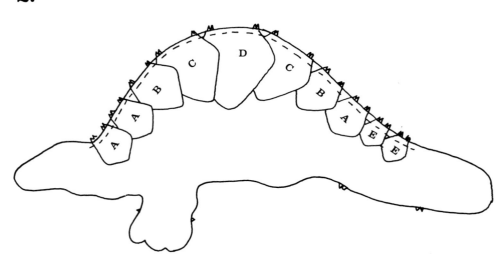

- Right side of body up, pin plates to body, noting plate size and position as shown on pattern. Pin plates to right side of body.
- Baste plates along seam line to body.
- Repeat for left side of body.
- Plates will alternate down the spine of the finished Stegosaurus. Note symbols on body pattern indicating placement of plates on right and left sides.

Plates alternate on spine.

〜〜〜〜〜〜
Plates on right side of body.

•〜〜〜〜〜•
Plates on left side of body.

3.

INSIDE LEG

INSIDE LEG

A
B

FOOT

OUTSIDE LEG

- Right sides together, matching notches, pin inside back leg and outside back leg together.
- Stitch around back leg from A to B, starting and stopping at circles.
- Repeat for remaining back leg.

- Right sides together, matching outside edges, pin back foot to bottom of back leg.
- Stitch foot to leg, starting and stopping at circles.
- Clip curves.
- Turn leg right side out through inside leg opening.
- Repeat for remaining back leg.

4.

- Right sides together, matching notches, pin back leg opening on body to inside back leg opening.
- Stitch back leg to body.
- Repeat for remaining back leg.

Stitch

BODY

FOOT

BACK LEG

5.

- Right sides facing, matching notches, pin right and left sides of the body together.
- Stitch as shown.
- Note: Back leg is not visible in illustration because right sides are together; the legs are sandwiched inside.

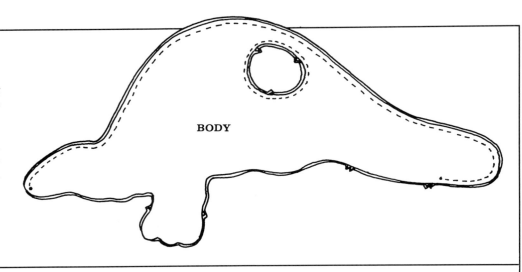

6.

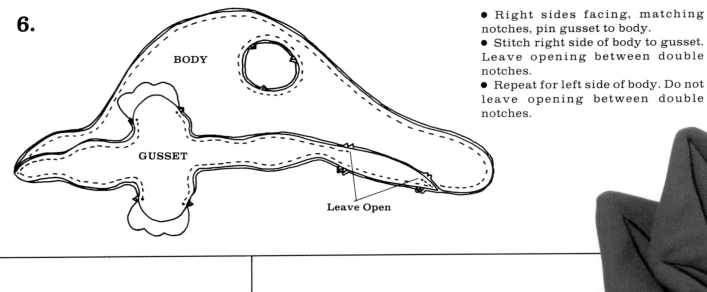

- Right sides facing, matching notches, pin gusset to body.
- Stitch right side of body to gusset. Leave opening between double notches.
- Repeat for left side of body. Do not leave opening between double notches.

7.

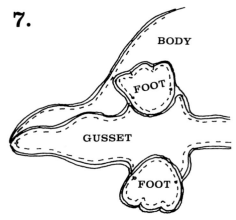

- Right sides together, matching outside edges, pin front feet to bottom of front legs.
- Stitch foot to leg.
- Repeat for remaining front leg.

- Clip curves on front legs, feet, and body.
- Turn body assembly right side out

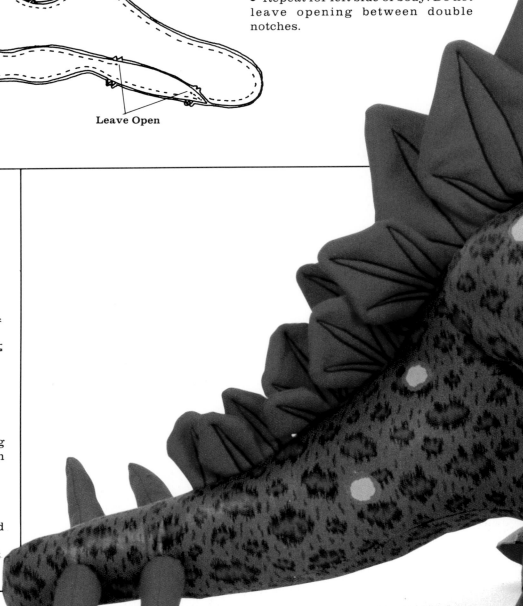

8.

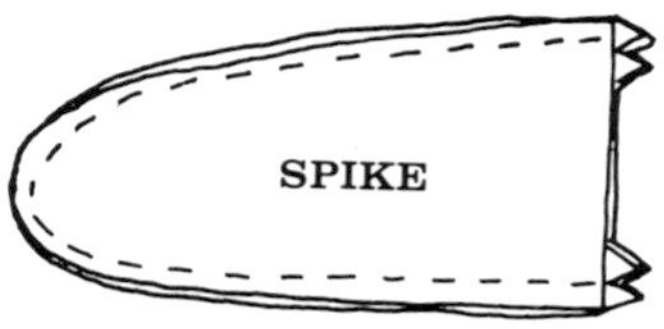

SPIKE

- Right sides together, pin two spike pieces together.
- Stitch from double notch to double notch as shown.
- Turn spike right side out.
- Repeat for remaining spike pieces.

- Apply eyes.

9.

- Stuff front feet and legs.
- Stuff back feet and legs.
- Stuff head and body.
- Stuff tail.

- Slipstitch tail opening closed.
- Stuff spikes.
- Turn under seam allowance on spikes, and stitch to tail in positions indicated.

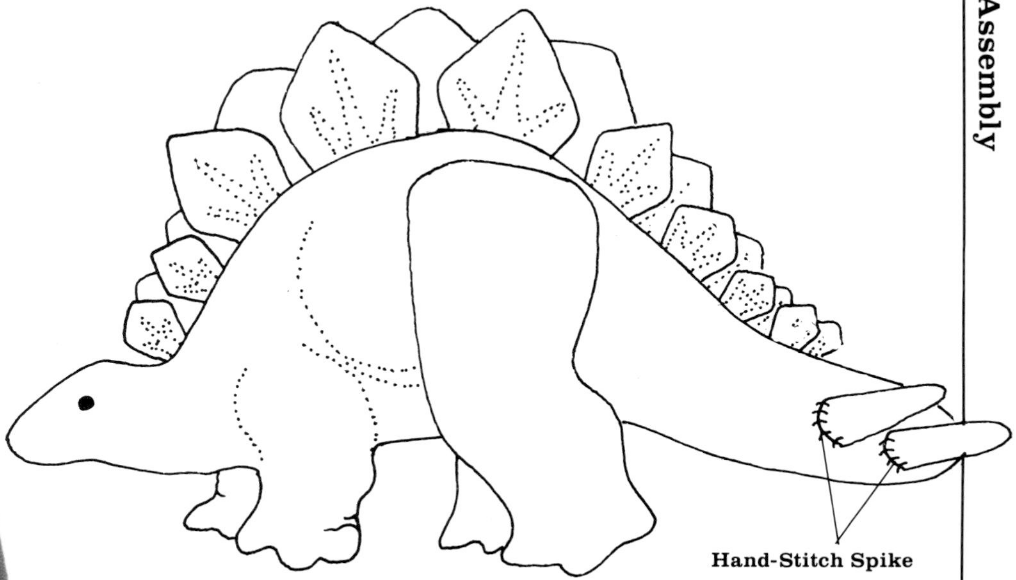

Hand-Stitch Spike

53

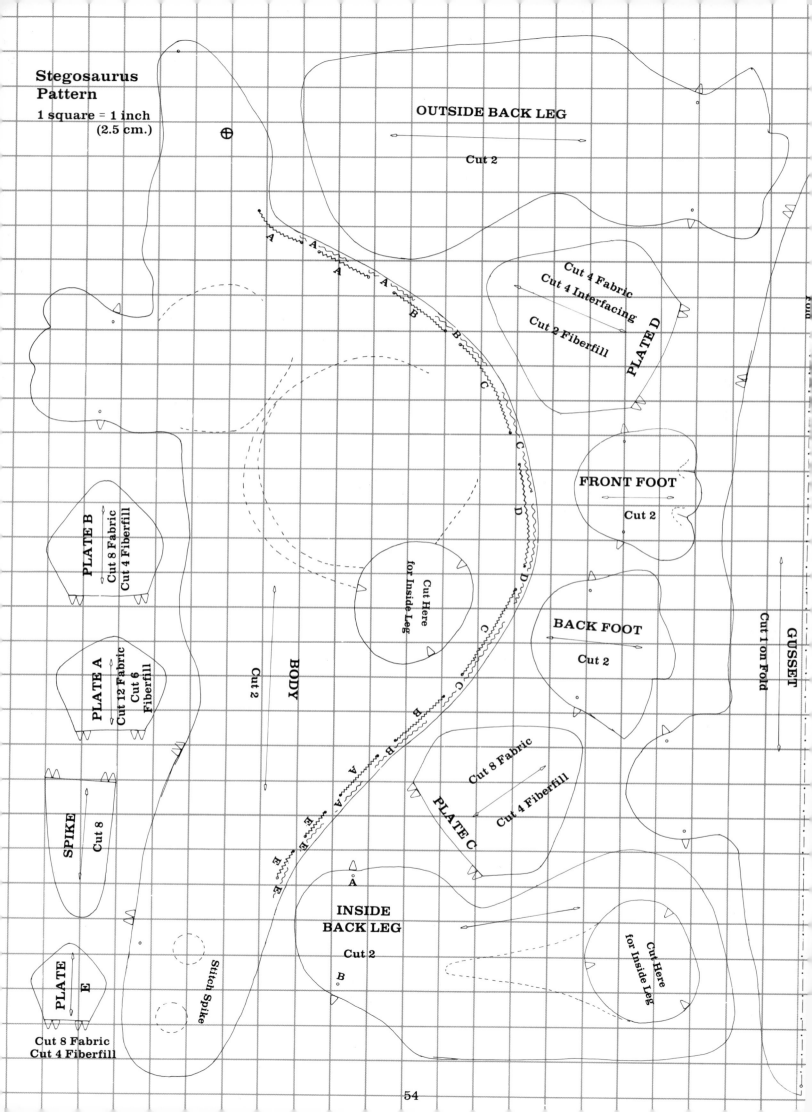

Stegosaurus
Pattern

1 square = 1 inch
(2.5 cm.)

OUTSIDE BACK LEG

Cut 2

PLATE D
Cut 4 Fabric
Cut 4 Interfacing
Cut 2 Fiberfill

FRONT FOOT
Cut 2

PLATE B
Cut 8 Fabric
Cut 4 Fiberfill

PLATE A
Cut 12 Fabric
Cut 6 Fiberfill

BODY
Cut 2

Cut Here
for Inside Leg

BACK FOOT
Cut 2

GUSSET
Cut 1 on Fold

PLATE C
Cut 8 Fabric
Cut 4 Fiberfill

SPIKE
Cut 8

INSIDE
BACK LEG

Cut 2

Stitch Spike

PLATE E

Cut 8 Fabric
Cut 4 Fiberfill

Cut Here
for Inside Leg

54

Triceratops and Stegosaurus Baby Dolls

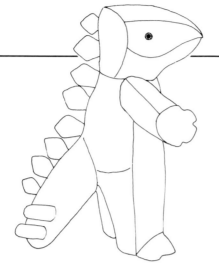

The emphasis in this book has been on realistic portrayals of dinosaurs. Why, then, are these anthropomorphic dinosaur dolls included? Well, there is something about them. Perhaps it was the look on my son's face when he first saw them, or perhaps it was because he said, "Hooray! A doll for a boy!"

The Triceratops pattern (above left) will sew a 20" (50 cm.) baby doll, which can wear size 12-months baby clothes.

The Stegosaurus doll was designed as a friend for the Triceratops. Since they were both vegetarians, they seemed ideal for each other. The body of the Stegosaurus doll is the same as that of the Triceratops.

This pattern will sew a 20" (50 cm.) Stegosaurus baby doll (which also wears size 12-months baby clothes).

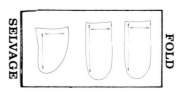

SEAM ALLOWANCE IS ¼" (6 mm.)

TRICERATOPS FABRIC REQUIREMENTS

The Triceratops doll seen in the photograph (on page 56) was sewn from a cotton-poly knit velour. This soft, stretchy fabric launders well and has an alluring softness that makes this doll very cuddly.

60" (150 cm.) fabric
Main color:
    1 yd. (90 cm.)
Horns:
    ⅛ yd. (11 cm.)

NOTIONS

Two 18 mm. safety-lock eyes
¼ yd. (23 cm.) heavyweight iron-on interfacing
Matching thread
1 lb. (2 kg.) polyester fiberfill stuffing
¼ yd. (23 cm.) polyester fiberfill batting

OPTIONAL

Mama box

TRICERATOPS PATTERN PIECES

1. BODY
2. HEAD GUSSET
3. HEAD BACK
4. COWL
5. COWL GUSSET
6. FRONT ARM
7. FRONT HAND
8. BACK ARM
9. FRONT BODY
10. FRONT FOOT
11. BACK BODY
12. BACK LEG
13. TAIL
14. HANDS
15. FEET
16. NOSE HORN
17. HORNS

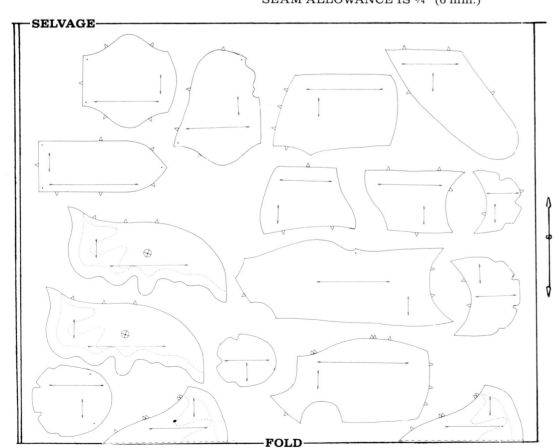

SELVAGE

FOLD

SELVAGE

FOLD

STEGOSAURUS FABRIC REQUIREMENTS

I sewed the Stegosaurus doll out of a cotton-poly velour knit to match Triceratops.

60″ (150 cm.) fabric
Main color:
¾ yd. (68 cm.)
Plates/spike color:
¼ yd. (23 cm.)

NOTIONS

Two 18 mm. plastic safety-lock eyes
Matching thread
1 lb. (½ kg.) polyester fiberfill stuffing
¼ yd. (23 cm.) heavyweight iron-on interfacing
¼ yd. (23 cm.) polyester fiberfill batting
Mama box or growler

SEAM ALLOWANCE IS ¼″ (6 mm.)

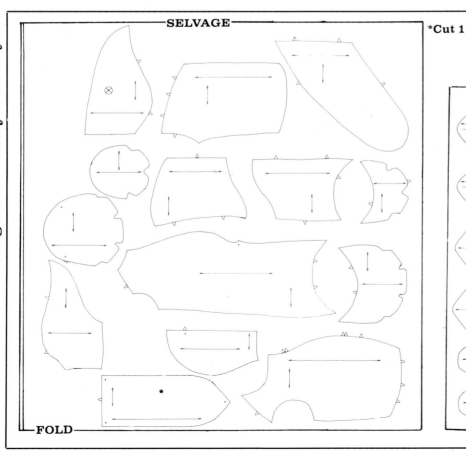

Stegosaurus Baby Doll Layout

SELVAGE

*Cut 1

SELVAGE

FOLD

FOLD

STEGOSAURUS PATTERN PIECES

1. LOWER HEAD
2. UPPER HEAD
3. HEAD BACK
4. GUSSET
5. FRONT ARM
6. FRONT HAND
7. BACK ARM
8. FRONT BODY
9. FRONT FOOT
10. BACK BODY
11. BACK LEG
12. TAIL
13. HAND
14. FEET
15. PLATE A
16. PLATE B
17. SPIKE

TRICERATOPS HEAD

1.

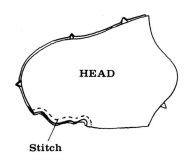

HEAD

Stitch

● Right sides together, matching notches, pin center front seam of head.
● Stitch; clip curves.

2.

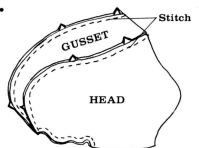

Stitch

GUSSET

HEAD

● Right sides together, matching notches, pin head gusset to right side of head.
● Repeat for left side of head to head gusset.
● Stitch; clip curves.

3.

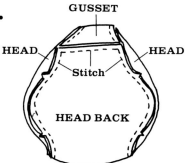

GUSSET

HEAD   HEAD

Stitch

HEAD BACK

● Right sides together, matching notches, pin head back to head/head gusset assembly.
● Stitch; clip curves.
● Turn head assembly right side out.

4.

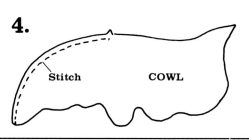

Stitch   COWL

● Right sides together, matching notches, pin center front seam of cowl.
● Stitch to notch as shown; clip curves.

5.

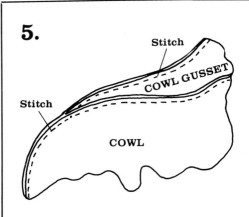

Stitch
COWL GUSSET
Stitch
COWL

- Right sides together, matching notches, pin cowl gusset to right side of cowl.
- Repeat for cowl gusset and left side of cowl.
- Stitch; clip curves.

6.

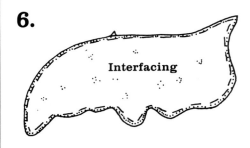

Interfacing

- Following manufacturer's directions, apply iron-on interfacing to cowl lining and cowl gusset lining.
- Baste cowl fiberfill and cowl gusset fiberfill to matching lining pieces.
- Assemble cowl lining as instructed for exterior cowl. Leave opening between double notches on right side of cowl.

7.

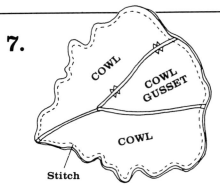

COWL
COWL GUSSET
COWL
Stitch

- Right sides together, matching edges and seams, pin cowl lining to cowl.
- Stitch around outside edge of cowl and cowl lining.
- Clip and trim seams. Turn right side out through opening in cowl lining. Press.
- Slipstitch opening in lining closed.

8.

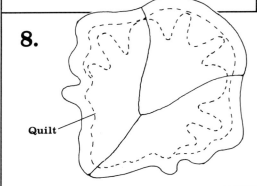

Quilt

- Topstitch ½″ (13 mm.) from outside edge of cowl.
- Machine stitch quilting pattern on cowl as shown.

- Apply eyes to cowl.

Go to body instructions, page 59.

STEGOSAURUS HEAD

1.

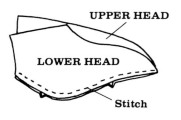

UPPER HEAD
LOWER HEAD
Stitch

- Right sides together, matching notches, pin upper head to lower head.
- Stitch as shown.
- Repeat for remaining upper and lower head.

2.

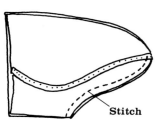

Stitch

- Right sides together, pin center front seam of head assembly together.
- Stitch as shown, starting at seam that joins upper and lower head.

3.

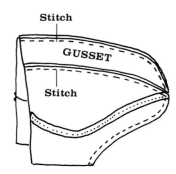

Stitch
GUSSET
Stitch

- Right sides together, pin head gusset to right side of upper head.
- Stitch. Clip curves.
- Repeat for left side of upper head to head gusset.

4.

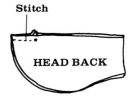

Stitch
HEAD BACK

- Right sides together, pin head-back together. Stitch from circle at notch to top of head as shown.

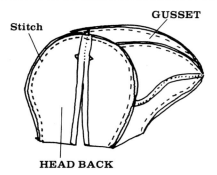

Stitch
GUSSET
Stitch
HEAD BACK

- Right sides together, pin head-back to head/head gusset assembly.
- Stitch. Clip curves.
- Turn head assembly right side out.

- Apply eyes.

Go to body instructions, page 59.

BODY (Both Dolls)

1.

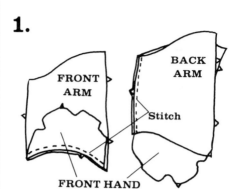

- Right sides together, matching notches and small circles, pin front hand to front arm.
- Stitch. Clip curves.
- Repeat for remaining front hand to front arm.

- Right sides together, matching notches, pin front arm assembly to back arm as shown.
- Stitch.
- Repeat for remaining front arm assembly and back arm.

2.

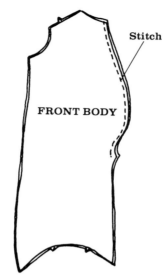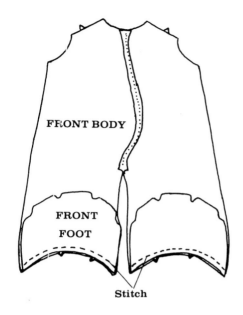

- Right sides together, pin center front seam of front body.
- Stitch from circle to neck.
- Stitch. Clip curves.

- Right sides together, matching notches and small circles, pin front foot to front body.
- Stitch; clip curves.
- Repeat for remaining front foot and front body.

3.

- Right sides together, matching notches, pin back leg to back body.
- Stitch; clip curves.
- Repeat for remaining back leg and back body.

4.

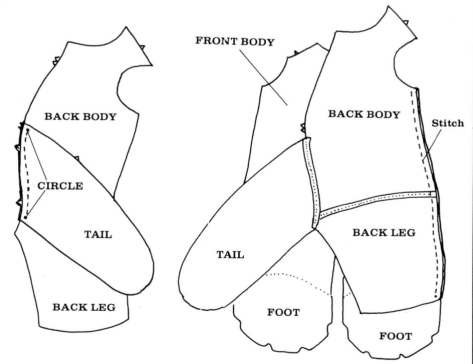

- Right sides together, matching notches and circles, pin tail to back of body/leg assembly.
- Stitch, starting and stopping at circles.
- Repeat for remaining tail to body/leg assembly.

- Right sides together, pin side seams of back assembly to front assembly.
- Stitch; clip curves.

59

5.

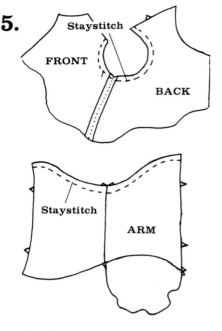

- Staystitch arm opening in body and top of arm as shown.

6.

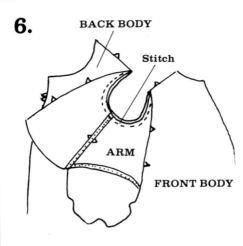

- Right sides together, matching notches, pin arm assembly to armhole edge of body front/back. Note: Underarm seam does not match.
- Stitch, easing arm to fit. Clip curves. To ease, use a medium-large stitch seam along seam line. Carefully pin and ease fabric to match.
- Repeat for remaining arm assembly to body assembly.

8A. STEGOSAURUS ONLY

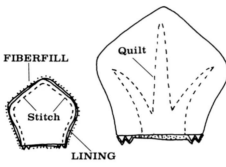

- Apply iron-on interfacing to all plate pieces.
- Right sides together, pin two plate pieces together.
- Match to piece of fiberfill, and pin sandwich of fabric and fiberfill together.
- Stitch as shown.
- Turn right side out through opening, and machine quilt.
- Repeat for all remaining plates.

9.

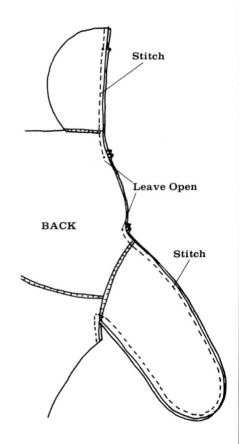

- Right sides together, matching notches, pin center back seam in body/tail, leaving an opening between double notches.
- Stitch center back and around tail.
- Clip curves.

Note that Triceratops head back is one piece; the back seam for that doll will start at the neck.

7.

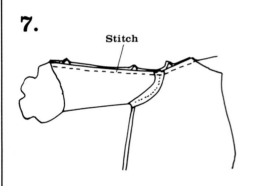

- Right sides together, matching notches and seams, pin arm/shoulder seams of front body to arm/shoulder seams of back body.
- Stitch.
- Repeat for remaining shoulder.

8.

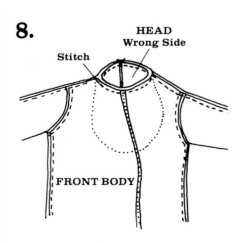

- Right sides together, matching notches and center seams, pin head assembly to body assembly.
- Stitch. Clip curves.

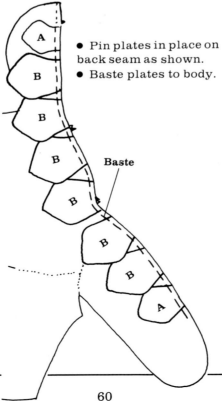

- Pin plates in place on back seam as shown.
- Baste plates to body.

10.

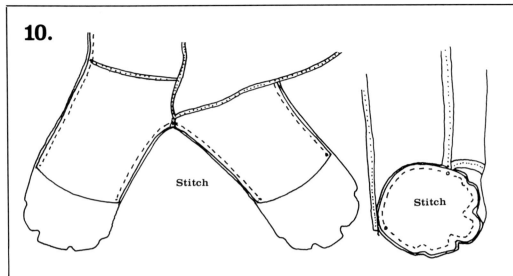

Stitch

Stitch

- Right sides together, pin inside leg seam. Stitch seam, and clip curve.

- Right sides together, matching notches, pin hand to opening in arm.
- Stitch following contours; clip curves.
- Repeat for remaining hand.
- Repeat for feet.

11.

OPTIONAL

- Stitch Mama box or growler in place on back seam.

- Turn doll right side out through back opening.

12.   Finishing Triceratops.

- Right sides together, matching notches, pin horn as shown.
- Stitch.
- Turn through opening.
- Repeat for remaining horns and nose horn.

- Stuff head.
- Stuff tail.
- Stuff the legs and arms.
- Stuff the remaining body.
- Slipstitch back body seam closed.
- Pin cowl assembly to head assembly, using circles to align.
- Hand-stitch cowl assembly to head assembly.
- Stuff horns firmly.
- Turn under seam allowance and hand-stitch horns to marked places on cowl.

12A.   Finishing Stegosaurus.

SPIKE

- Right sides together, pin two spike pieces together.
- Stitch.
- Turn through opening.
- Repeat for remaining spikes.

- Stuff head.
- Stuff tail.
- Stuff legs and arms.
- Stuff the remaining body.
- Slipstitch back body seam closed.
- Stuff spikes firmly.
- Turn under seam allowance and hand-stitch spikes to tail.

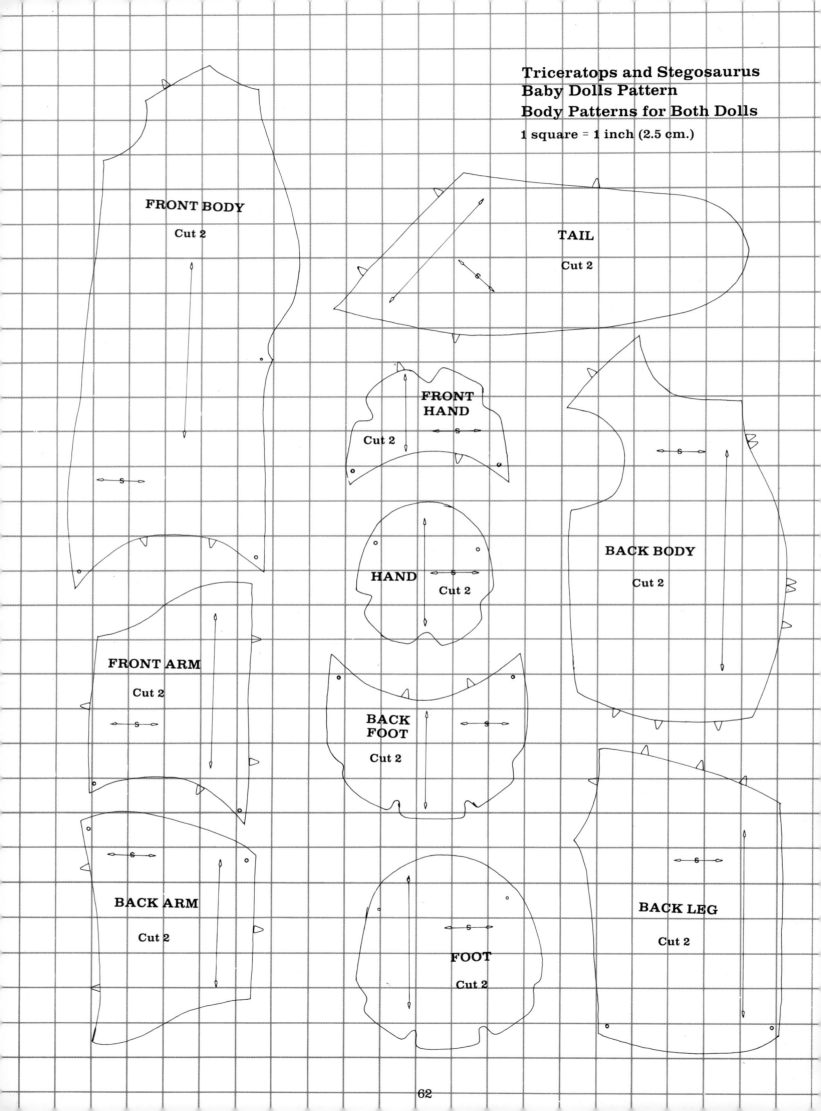

Triceratops and Stegosaurus
Baby Dolls Pattern
Body Patterns for Both Dolls

1 square = 1 inch (2.5 cm.)

FRONT BODY

Cut 2

TAIL

Cut 2

FRONT
HAND

Cut 2

BACK BODY

Cut 2

HAND

Cut 2

FRONT ARM

Cut 2

BACK
FOOT

Cut 2

BACK ARM

Cut 2

BACK LEG

Cut 2

FOOT

Cut 2

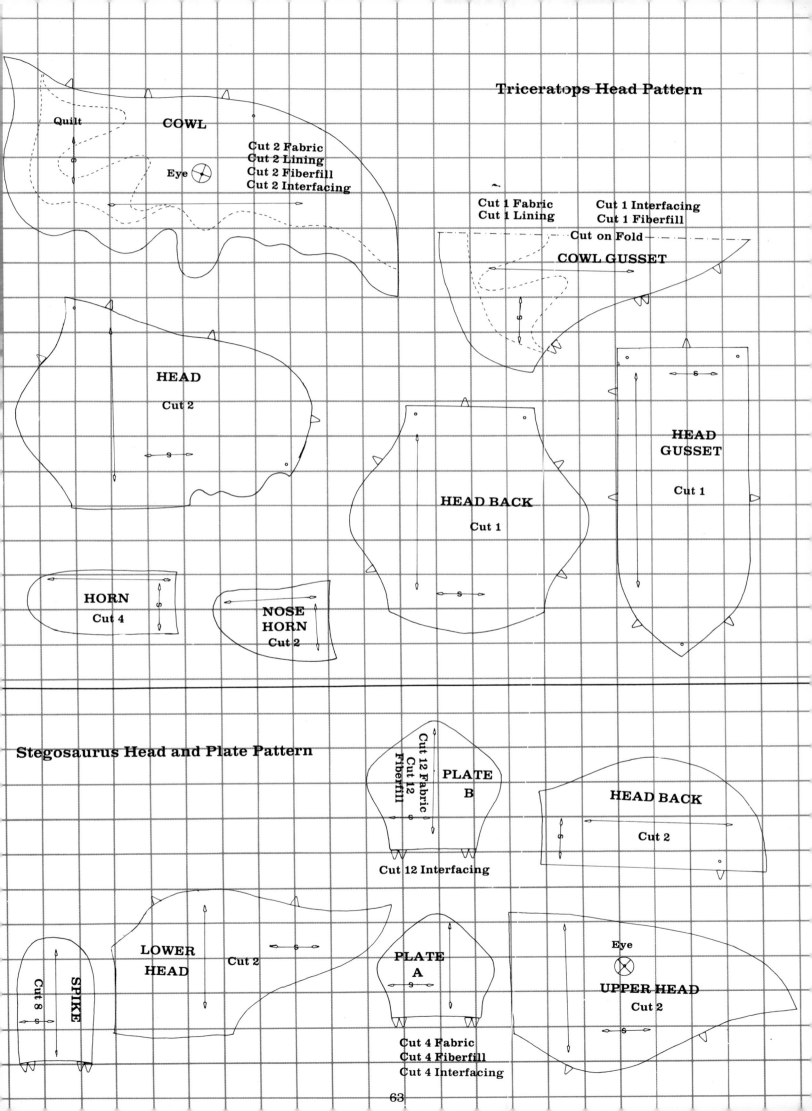

Triceratops Head Pattern

Quilt

COWL

Cut 2 Fabric
Cut 2 Lining
Cut 2 Fiberfill
Cut 2 Interfacing

Eye

Cut 1 Fabric   Cut 1 Interfacing
Cut 1 Lining   Cut 1 Fiberfill

— Cut on Fold —

COWL GUSSET

HEAD

Cut 2

HEAD GUSSET

Cut 1

HEAD BACK

Cut 1

HORN

Cut 4

NOSE HORN

Cut 2

Stegosaurus Head and Plate Pattern

Cut 12 Fabric
Cut 12 Fiberfill

PLATE B

Cut 12 Interfacing

HEAD BACK

Cut 2

LOWER HEAD

Cut 2

SPIKE

Cut 8

PLATE A

Cut 4 Fabric
Cut 4 Fiberfill
Cut 4 Interfacing

Eye

UPPER HEAD

Cut 2

Spinosaurus

Spinosaurus

Spinosaurus (spine-o-SORE-us) lived during the late Cretaceous period. This strange, meat-eating dinosaur grew to be about 40 feet (12 meters) long and had a sail made from skin on his back, which he may have used to control his body temperature, much as Dimetrodon did. Spinosaurus fossils have been found in Egypt.

This pattern sews a model of Spinosaurus 21″ (53 cm.) long.

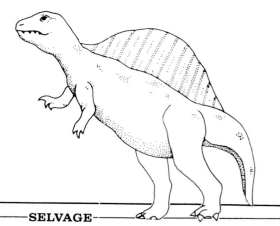

FABRIC REQUIREMENTS

This dinosaur was sewn from suede cloth. Because I found the color a little dull, I decided to enliven the skin with machine embroidery. Many different shades of brown and yellow thread produced a lively look.

45″ (112 cm.) fabric
Main color:
1 yd. (90 cm.)

NOTIONS

Two 15 mm. cat's-eye plastic safety eyes
Two 55 mm. plastic joints
Two 65 mm. plastic joints
1 lb. (2 kg.) polyester fiberfill stuffing
¼ yd. (23 cm.) heavyweight iron-on interfacing
¼ yd. (23 cm.) polyester fiberfill batting
Matching thread

SEAM ALLOWANCE IS ¼″ (6 mm.)

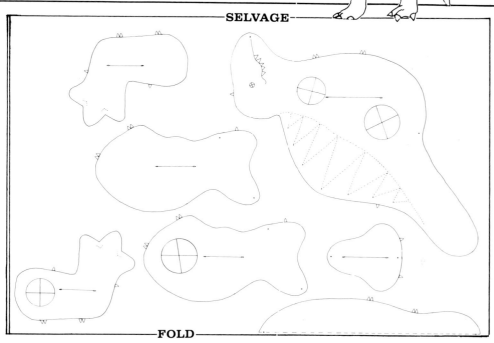

SELVAGE

FOLD

PATTERN PIECES

1. BODY   4. FOOT
2. GUSSET   5. ARM
3. LEG   6. SAIL (Interfacing and batting)

1.

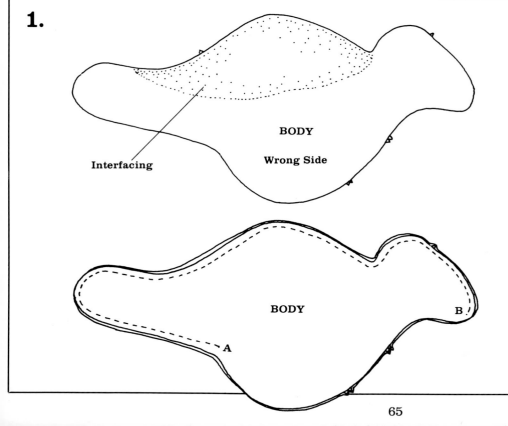

Interfacing

BODY
Wrong Side

BODY

BODY

A

B

• Following manufacturer's instructions, apply interfacing to wrong side of sail portion of body pieces.

• Right sides together, matching notches, pin body pieces together. Stitch from A to B, starting and stopping at circles.

65

2.

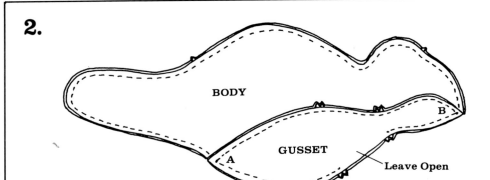

● Right sides together, matching notches, pin gusset to the right side of the body. Baste. Stitch from A to B. Leave opening between double notches.

● Repeat for gusset to left side of body. Do not leave opening between double notches.
● Clip curves and trim seams.
● Turn body right side out through opening in tail.
● Press.

3.

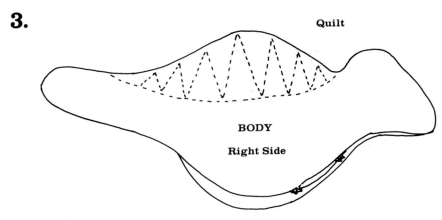

● Place fiberfill batting sail inside of body as shown. Baste through both layers of fabric and fiberfill. Machine quilt along marked lines on sail.

4.

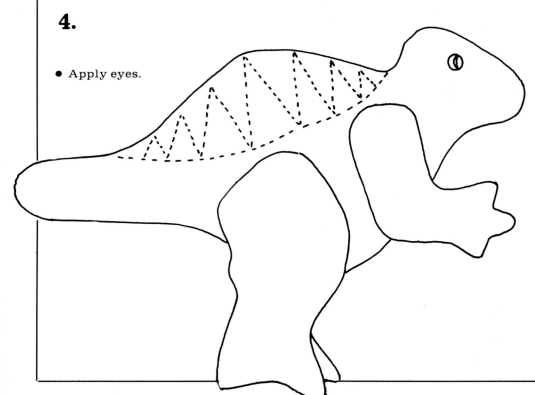

● Apply eyes.

5.

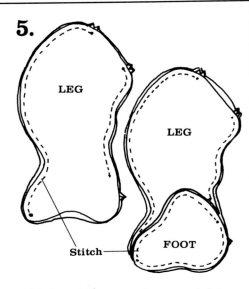

● Right sides together, matching notches, pin two leg pieces together.
● Stitch; leave opening between double notches. Start and stop at circles as shown.
● Repeat for remaining leg pieces.

● Right sides together, matching outside edges, pin foot to bottom of leg.
● Stitch foot to leg.
● Clip curves on leg and foot.
● Turn leg/foot right side out through opening.
● Repeat for remaining leg and foot.

6.

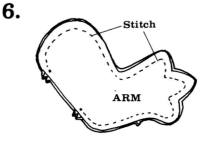

● Right sides together, matching notches, pin two arm pieces together.
● Stitch, leaving opening between double notches.
● Repeat for remaining arm pieces.

7.

● Using plastic joints, apply arms to body at markings.
● Repeat for joining legs to body.

8.

● Stuff arms.
● Slipstitch arm opening closed.
● Stuff legs.
● Slipstitch leg openings closed.
● Stuff head.
● Stuff tail.
● Stuff body.
● Slipstitch body opening closed.

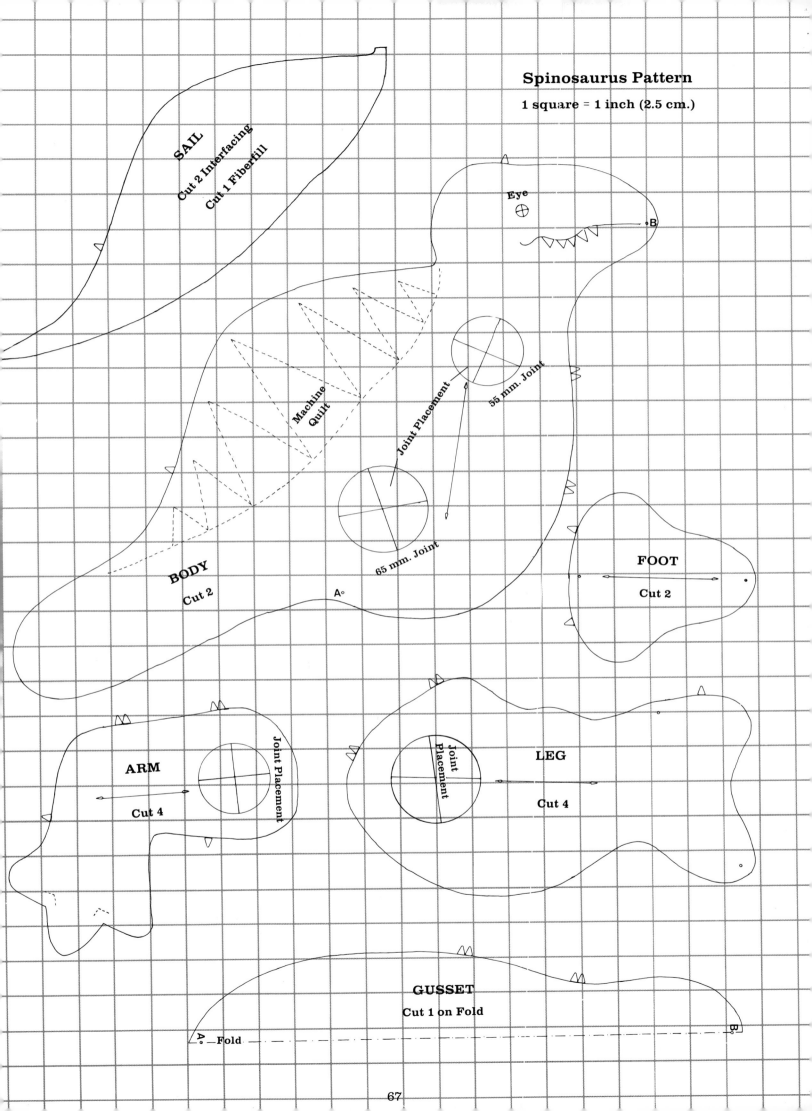

Spinosaurus Pattern

1 square = 1 inch (2.5 cm.)

SAIL
Cut 2 Interfacing
Cut 1 Fiberfill

Eye

B

Machine Quilt

Joint Placement

55 mm. Joint

65 mm. Joint

BODY
Cut 2

A

FOOT
Cut 2

ARM
Cut 4

Joint Placement

Joint Placement

LEG
Cut 4

GUSSET
Cut 1 on Fold

A — Fold

B

At 40 feet (12 meters) long, Spinosaurus was an enormous dinosaur. Her sail, which was taller than a man, made Spinosaurus unusually heavy. With a weight estimated at seven tons (six metric tons), she was almost as heavy as Tyrannosaurus Rex, the largest carnivore of all.

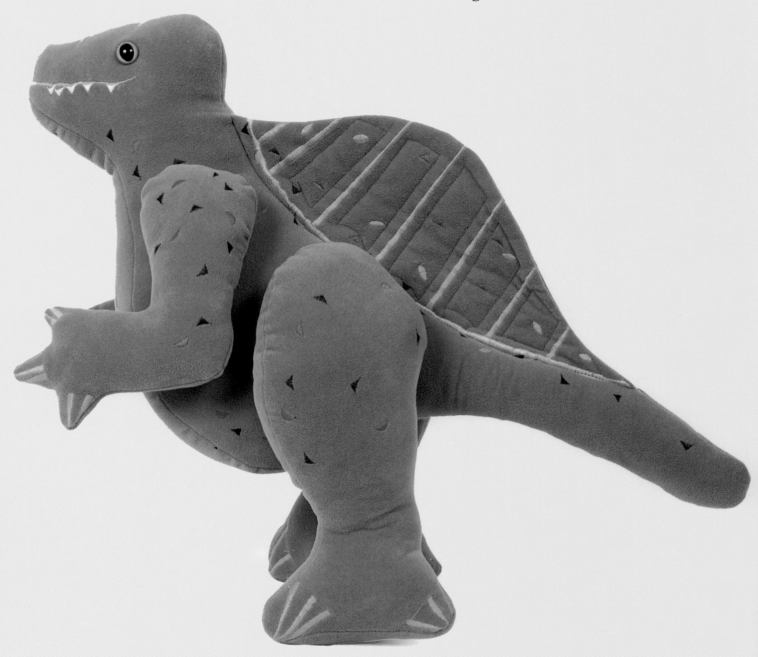

Eryops

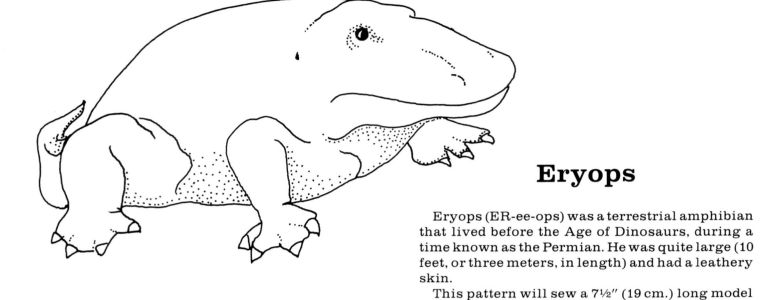

Eryops

Eryops (ER-ee-ops) was a terrestrial amphibian that lived before the Age of Dinosaurs, during a time known as the Permian. He was quite large (10 feet, or three meters, in length) and had a leathery skin.

This pattern will sew a 7½″ (19 cm.) long model of Eryops.

FABRIC REQUIREMENTS

I used a cotton broadcloth fabric to sew Eryops and large decorative buttons for eyes. If this were to be a toy for a small child, I would replace the buttons with safety eyes.

45″ (112 cm.) fabric
Main color:
    ¼ yd. (23 cm.)

NOTIONS

Two 9 mm. safety eyes
Matching thread
4 oz. (113 g.) polyester fiberfill
    stuffing

PATTERN PIECES

1. HEAD
2. MIDDLE
3. TAIL
4. GUSSET

 SEAM ALLOWANCE IS ¼″ (6 mm.)

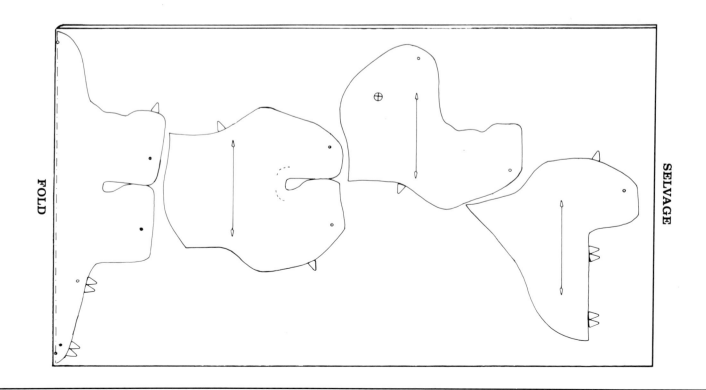

FOLD

SELVAGE

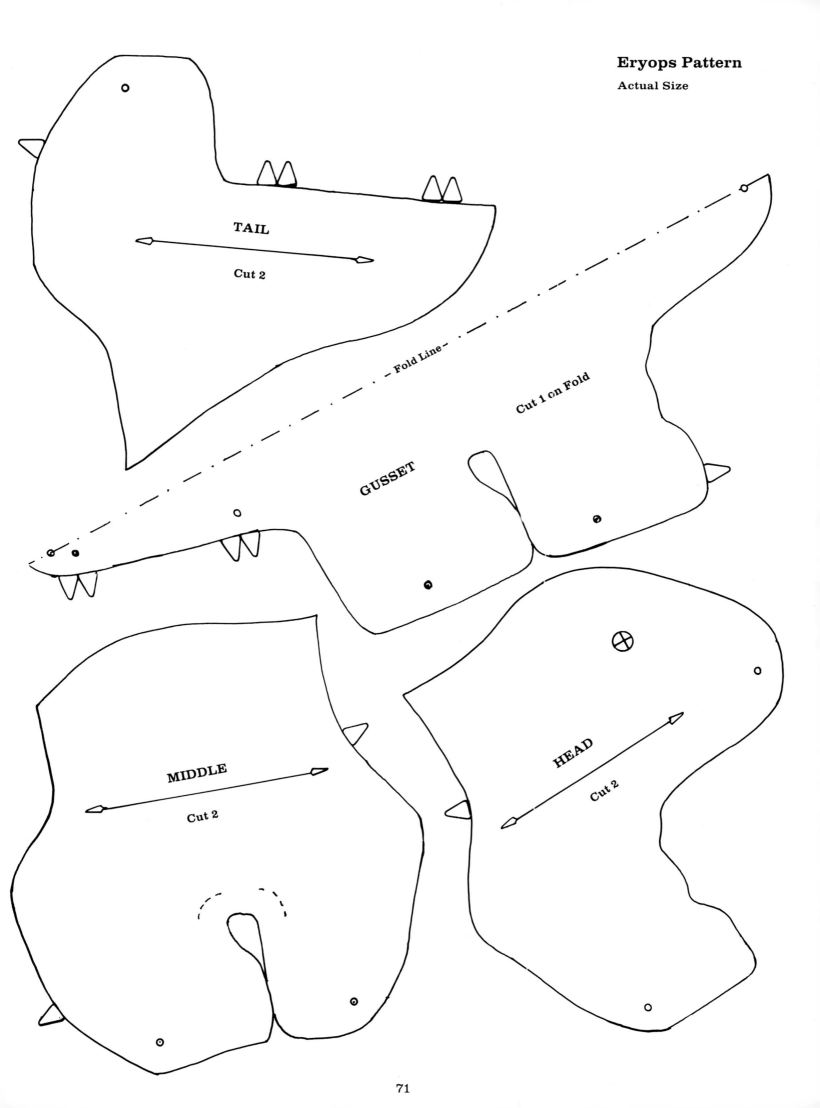

Eryops Pattern

Actual Size

TAIL

Cut 2

Fold Line

Cut 1 on Fold

GUSSET

MIDDLE

Cut 2

HEAD

Cut 2

1.

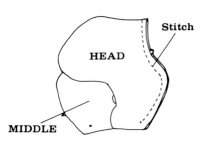

- Right sides together, matching notches, pin head to middle. Stitch, starting and stopping at circles.
- Press.
- Repeat for remaining head to middle.

2.

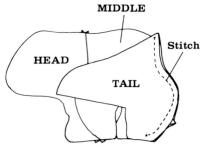

- Right sides together, matching notches, pin middle to tail. Stitch, starting and stopping at circles.
- Press.
- Repeat for remaining middle to tail.

3.

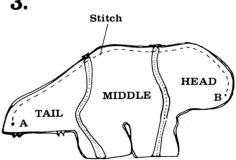

- Right sides together, matching notches and seams, pin body assemblies together, as shown. Stitch from A to B.

4.

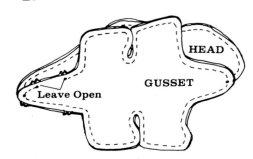

- Right sides together, matching notches and circles, pin right half of body to gusset. Stitch, starting and stopping at circles. Be careful at seams joining body piece not to catch seam allowances.
- Repeat for left side of body and gusset. Leave opening between double notches.

5.

- Turn Eryops right side out through opening.

- Apply eyes.

- Stuff legs.
- Stuff head.
- Stuff body.
- Stuff tail.
- Slipstitch opening closed.

Ankylosaurus

Ankylosaurus

Ankylosaurus (an-kee-lo-SORE-us) was a plant eater who lived during the late Cretaceous period. Over 32 feet (10 meters) long and 10 feet (three meters) wide, he had an armor of spines, knobs, and spikes on his body. His tail was long and carried a heavy club of bone at the end.

This pattern will sew a 10½″ (26 cm.) long realistic model of Ankylosaurus.

Ankylosaurus Layout

FABRIC REQUIREMENTS

Use any lightweight to medium weight, firmly woven fabric.

45″ (112 cm.) fabric
Main color:
½ yd. (45 cm.)

NOTIONS

Two 9 mm. safety eyes
4 oz. (113 g.) polyester fiberfill
    stuffing
Matching thread

PATTERN PIECES

1. BODY
2. GUSSET
3. SIDE

SEAM ALLOWANCE IS ¼″ (6 mm.)

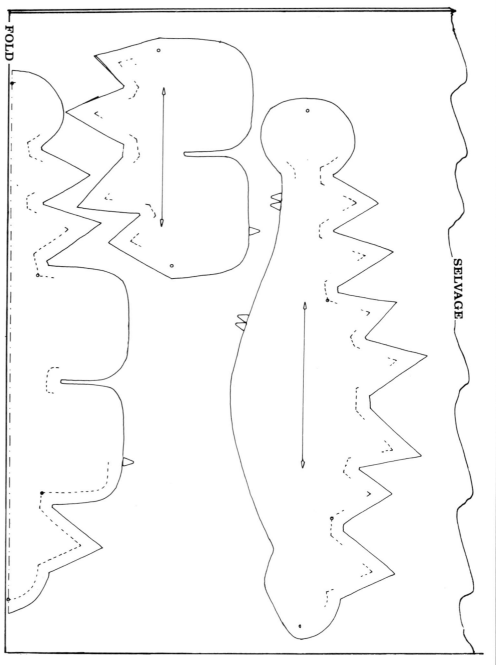

FOLD

SELVAGE

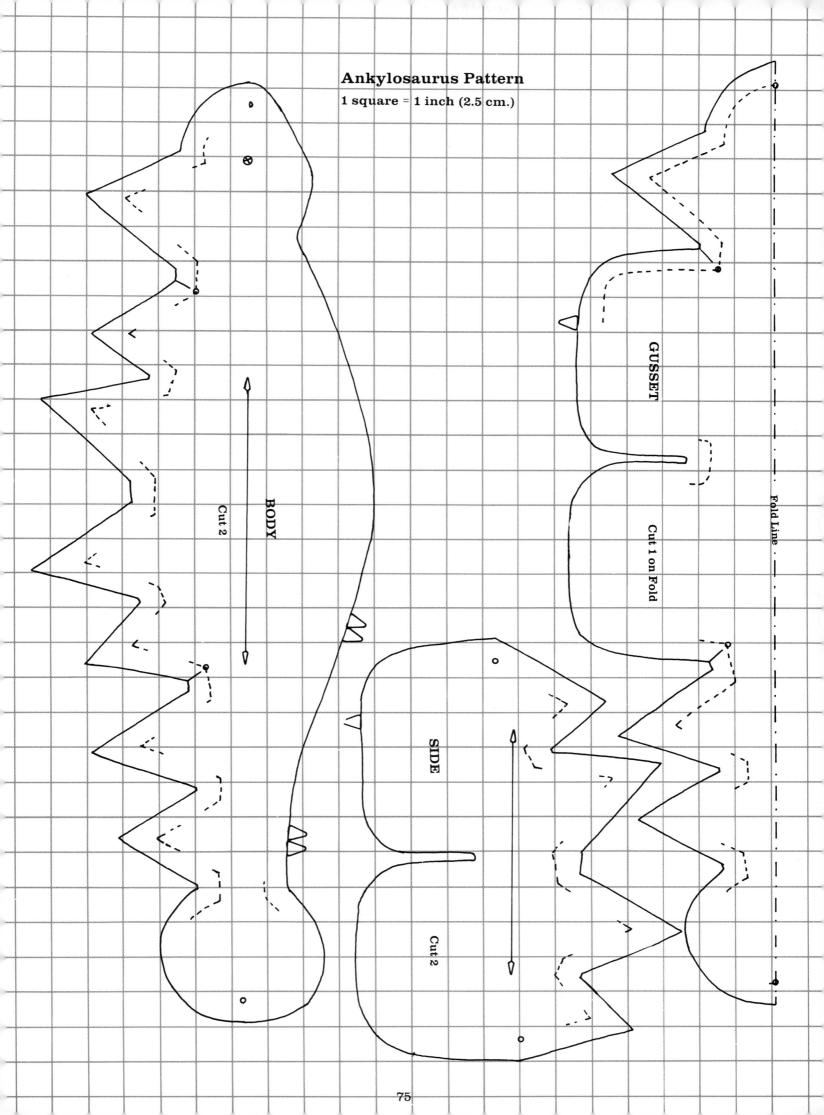

Ankylosaurus Pattern
1 square = 1 inch (2.5 cm.)

GUSSET

Cut 1 on Fold

Fold Line

BODY

Cut 2

SIDE

Cut 2

1.

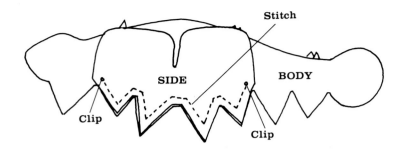

- Right sides together, matching outside edges, pin side piece to body. Stitch from circle to circle. Use stitching line marked on pattern for accuracy.
- Clip as shown.
- Repeat for remaining side and body pieces.

2.

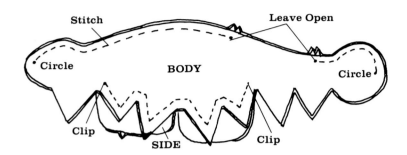

- Right sides together, matching notches, pin right and left body assemblies together along back. Stitch, starting and stopping at circles as shown. Leave opening between double notches.

3.

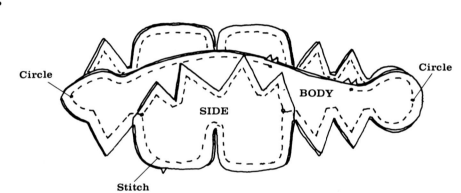

- Right sides together, matching notches, pin gusset to body assembly. Stitch, starting and stopping at circles.
- Clip curves and trim points.
- Carefully turn Ankylosaurus right side out.

- Apply eyes.

- Stuff head and points.
- Stuff legs.
- Stuff body.
- Stuff tail.
- Slipstitch opening on body closed.

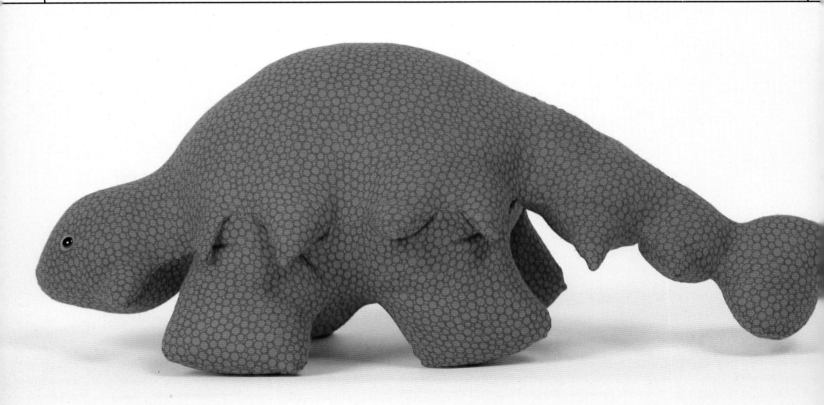

Tyrannosaurus Rex

Tyrannosaurus Rex

Tyrannosaurus Rex (tie-ran-o-SORE-us rex), the "tyrant lizard king," is believed to be the largest predator that ever stalked the earth. Its body measured 40 feet (12 meters) from head to tail. Tyrannosaurus was 20 feet (six meters) tall and weighed about eight tons (seven metric tons). This huge meat-eater was king of the beasts 65 million years ago; he lived during the late Cretaceous. Fossils have been found in North America and Asia. It is thought that Tyrannosaurus may have eaten mostly Hadrosaurs.

This pattern will sew a 27″ (63 cm.) tall realistic model of this ferocious dinosaur.

FABRIC REQUIREMENTS

Tyrannosaurus was a mean and frightening reptile. He could probably swallow human beings whole if he were alive today. I have chosen a deep color to convey the dark side of his behavior.

I used a fabric paint to add claws in a contrast color on Tyrannosaurus Rex. Yellow, brown, black, and beige are all very believable claw colors. I avoid using white, as it produces a dainty look—which is out of character for him.

45″ (112 cm.) fabric
Main color:
    1¾ yds. (158 cm.)
Belly/eye color:
    ⅛ yd. (11 cm.)
Teeth color:
    ⅛ yd. (11 cm.)

NOTIONS

Two 19 mm. safety eyes.
3 lbs. (1½ kg.) polyester fiberfill stuffing
Matching thread
Two 55 mm. movable joints (arms)

PATTERN PIECES

1. BODY
2. TEETH
3. JAW
4. HEAD
5. EYELID
6. EYEBALL
7. STOMACH
8. CHEST
9. GUSSET
10. INSIDE TOE
11. OUTSIDE TOE
12. LEG
13. ARM

SEAM ALLOWANCE IS ¼″ (6 mm.)

SELVAGE

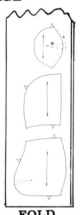

FOLD   **FOLD**

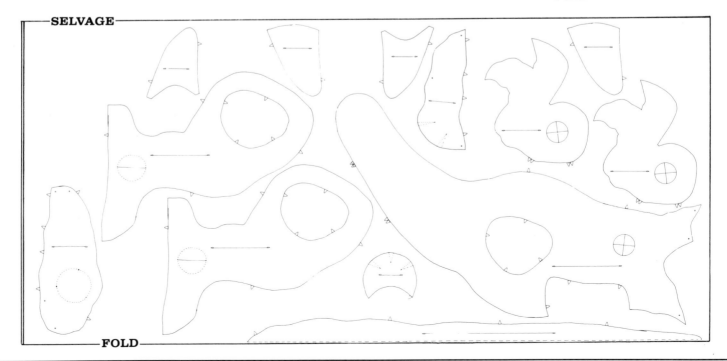

SELVAGE

FOLD

1.

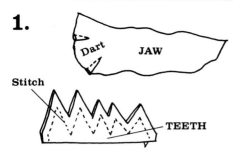

- To make each dart in jaw, fold on dot-dashed line, right sides together.
- Pin and stitch along dashed line.

- Right sides together, pin two teeth pieces together. Stitch, using a very small, tight stitch. Trim teeth closely and turn right side out carefully. Press.
- Repeat for remaining teeth.

2.

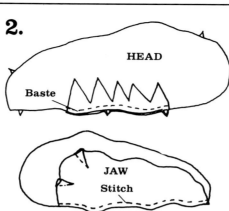

- Right sides together, matching notches, pin teeth to head. Baste.
- Repeat for remaining teeth.

- Right sides together, matching notches, fit jaw and head together; pin.
- Stitch as shown.
- Clip curves.

- Press teeth toward jaw. Zigzag or topstitch seam as shown.

3.

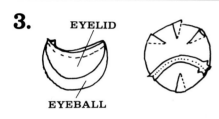

- Staystitch notched edge of eyelid. Clip to help in fitting to eyeball.
- Right sides together, matching notches, pin eyeball and eyelid together. Baste.
- Stitch.

- Fold each dart on eyelid and eyeball along fold line, right sides together. Stitch along dashed line.
- Turn eye assembly right side out.

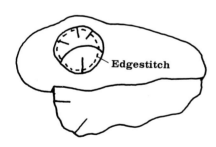

- Turn under seam allowance on eye assembly, and pin to marked area on head. Match seams to circles marked on head. Baste.
- Edgestitch eye assembly to head.

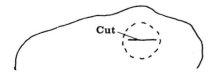

- Carefully cut slit on body inside eye stitching line to allow the installation of a plastic eye and stuffing into eye assembly at a later time.

4.

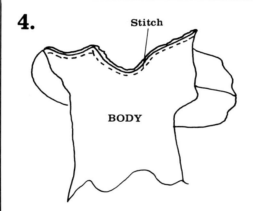

- Right sides together, matching notches and circles, fit body to head/jaw assembly. Pin and baste.
- Stitch.
- Clip curves.

5.

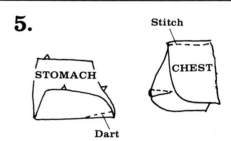

- Fold dart in stomach along dot-dashed line, right sides together. Stitch along dashed lines.

- Right sides together, matching notches, pin chest and stomach together.
- Stitch.

6.

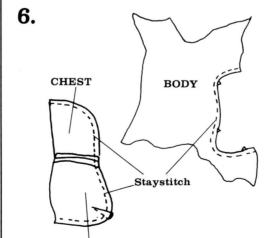

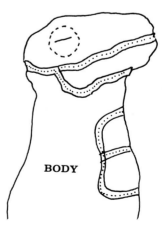

- Staystitch opening in body.
- Clip at corners.

- Staystitch opening in stomach/chest.

- Right sides together, matching notches, fit stomach/chest to body. Pin and baste.
- Stitch.

7.

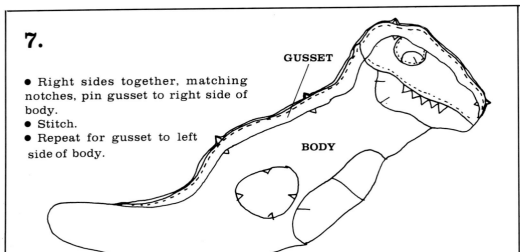

- Right sides together, matching notches, pin gusset to right side of body.
- Stitch.
- Repeat for gusset to left side of body.

8.

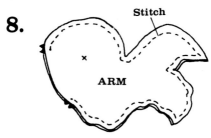

- Right sides together, pin two arm pieces together.
- Stitch from double notch to double notch. Leave opening between double notches.
- Clip curves.
- Turn arm right side out.
- Repeat for remaining arm pieces.

9.

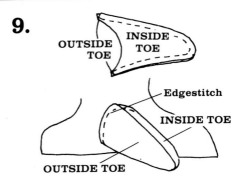

- Right sides together, pin inside toe and outside toe together.
- Stitch from double notch to double notch. Leave opening between double notches.
- Clip curves.
- Turn toe right side out.
- Staystitch unfinished edge of toe.
- Repeat for remaining toes.
- Turn under seam allowance on unfinished edge of toe.

- Pin toes in place on leg, matching seams to marks on leg. Baste.
- Edgestitch toes to legs.
- Repeat for remaining toes.

10.

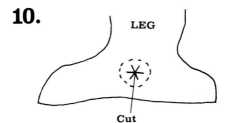

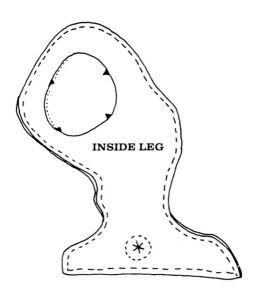

- Carefully cut slit in leg to allow for stuffing to be inserted in toes.

- Right sides together, pin outside leg and inside leg pieces together.
- Arrange the toes so they will not get caught in the seam.
- Stitch around the leg.
- Clip curves.
- Turn leg right side out through opening in inside leg.
- Repeat for remaining inside leg and outside leg.

11.

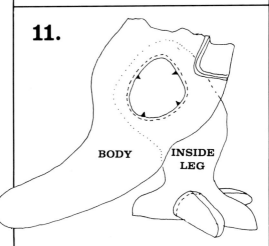

- Right sides together, matching notches, pin leg opening on body to opening on inside leg.
- Stitch leg to body.
- Repeat for remaining leg.

12.

- Right sides together, matching notches, pin remaining seams on body halves together. Stitch. Leave opening between double notches.

- Apply eyes.
- Stuff eye assembly firmly. Hand-stitch opening closed. Do not pull opening too tight, or eye assembly will distort.
- Attach arms, using plastic movable joints.
- Stuff arms. Slipstitch openings closed.
- Stuff toes.
- Stuff legs.
- Stuff head and body.
- Stuff tail.
- Baste body opening closed.
- Slipstitch body opening closed.

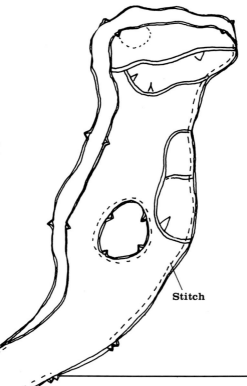

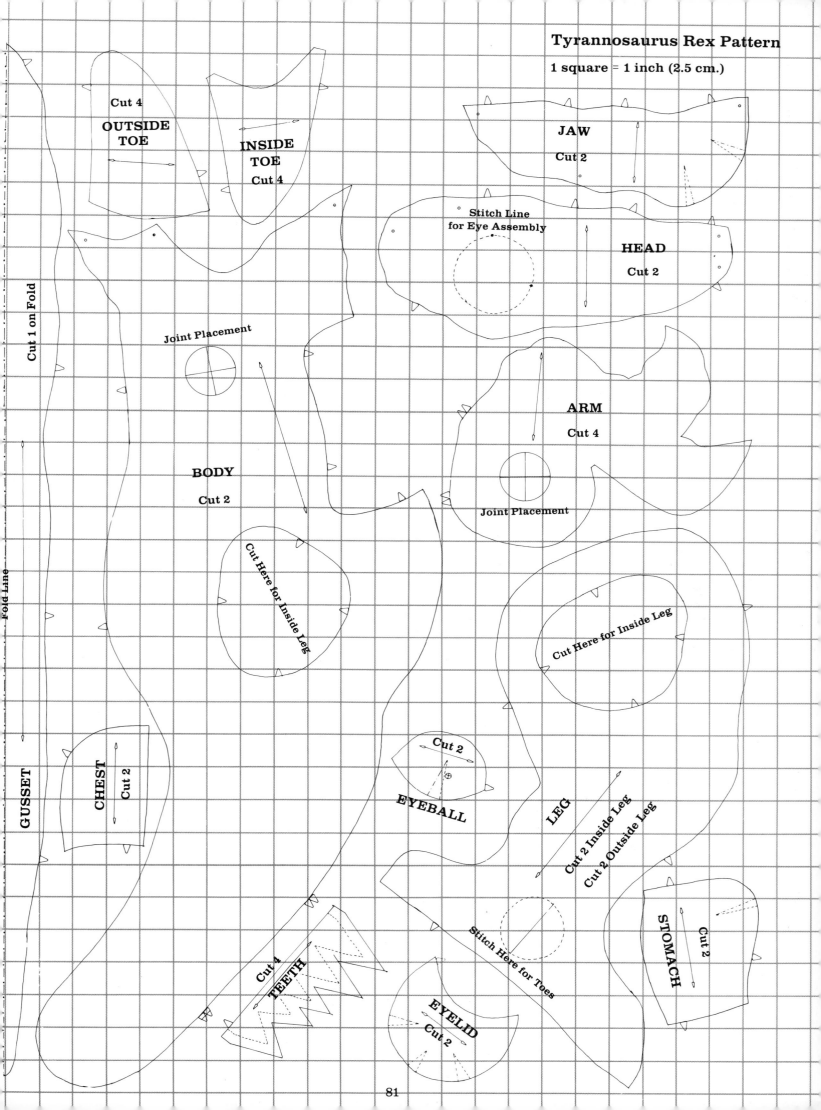

Tyrannosaurus Rex Pattern

1 square = 1 inch (2.5 cm.)

Cut 4
OUTSIDE TOE

INSIDE TOE
Cut 4

JAW
Cut 2

Stitch Line
for Eye Assembly

HEAD
Cut 2

Cut 1 on Fold

Joint Placement

ARM
Cut 4

BODY
Cut 2

Joint Placement

Cut Here for Inside Leg

Cut Here for Inside Leg

Fold Line

Cut 2

GUSSET

CHEST
Cut 2

EYEBALL

LEG
Cut 2 Inside Leg
Cut 2 Outside Leg

Stitch Here for Toes

STOMACH
Cut 2

Cut 4
TEETH

EYELID
Cut 2

Dimetrodon

Dimetrodon

Dimetrodon (die-MET-ro-don) was not a dinosaur but a member of the paramammals, a prehistoric group that lived before the dinosaurs. When the dinosaurs evolved, these primitive, mammal-like reptiles disappeared.

Dimetrodon was about 10 feet (three meters) long and weighed about 440 pounds (200 kilograms). It is believed that the large sail on its back helped Dimetrodon control its temperature. The sail was supported by long spikes growing from the backbone and was covered in skin. Dimetrodon fossils have been found in North America.

This pattern will sew a 10″ (25 cm.) long model of this prehistoric beast.

Dimetrodon Layout

FABRIC REQUIREMENTS

Dimetrodon is quick and easy to sew. Make several in lots of colors. All surface design techniques work well on Dimetrodon—which means he's lots of fun.

45″ (112 cm.) fabric

Main color:
½ yd. (45 cm.)

SEAM ALLOWANCE IS ¼″ (6 mm.)

NOTIONS

Two 9mm. safety eyes
4 oz. (113 g.) polyester fiberfill stuffing
4 ½″ x 8″ (11 x 20 cm.) polyester fiberfill batting
Matching thread

PATTERN PIECES

1. BODY
2. GUSSET
3. SAIL (batting)

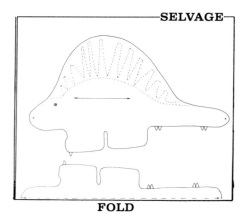

SELVAGE

FOLD

Dimetrodon Assembly

1.

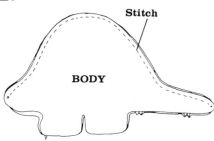

Stitch

BODY

● Right sides together, matching notches, pin body pieces together. Stitch, starting and stopping at circles.

2.

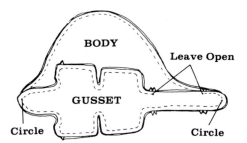

BODY

Leave Open

GUSSET

Circle   Circle

● Right sides together, matching notches, pin gusset to the right side of the body. Baste. Stitch, starting and stopping at circles. Leave opening between double notches.
● Repeat for gusset to left side of body. Do not leave opening between double notches.
● Clip curves and trim seams.
● Turn body right side out through opening in tail.

3.

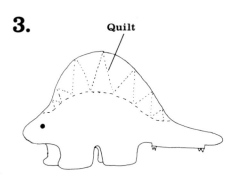

Quilt

● Place fiberfill batting sail inside of body as shown. Baste through both layers of fabric and fiberfill. Machine quilt along lines marked on sail.

● Apply eyes.
● Stuff legs.
● Stuff head.
● Stuff body.
● Slipstitch opening in tail closed.

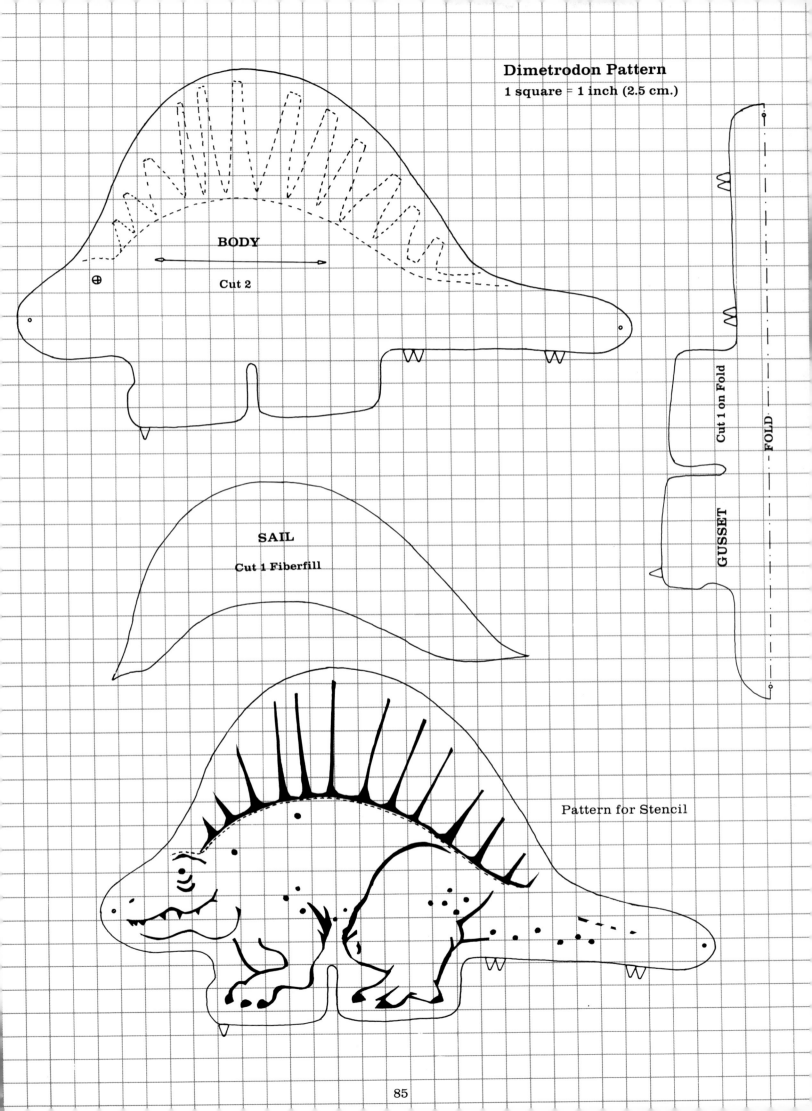

Dimetrodon Pattern

1 square = 1 inch (2.5 cm.)

BODY

Cut 2

SAIL

Cut 1 Fiberfill

Cut 1 on Fold

GUSSET

FOLD

Pattern for Stencil

85

Protoceratops Hatchling

Protoceratops Hatchling

Discoveries of Protoceratops (pro-toe-SER-a-tops) eggs were made in the 1920s in Mongolia. Some eggs were discovered laid in a circle in the nest. It is presumed that the mother dug a bowl-shaped nest, laid her eggs, and covered them with earth to protect them until they hatched. An adult Protoceratops was six feet (almost two meters) long, yet the eggs were a mere eight inches (20 centimeters) long.

This pattern will sew a 9″ (23 cm.) model of baby Protoceratops and egg.

FABRIC REQUIREMENTS

This dinosaur seems to love bright colors. Try sewing it with a solid for the body, cowl, legs, and arms, and matching prints for the belly and footpads. Construct the outside of the egg from quilted fabric to give structure to the shape. Although it is easiest to use quilted fabric for the egg, you can also custom quilt fabric. Just place fiberfill between fabric and lining and machine quilt in desired pattern.

45″ (112 cm.) fabric
Main color:
  ¼ yd. (23 cm.)
Contrast color:
  ¼ yd. (23 cm.)
Egg (outside):
  18″ x 22″ (45 x 55 cm.)
  quilted fabric
Egg (lining):
  18″ x 22″ (45 x 55 cm.)

NOTIONS

Two 9 mm. safety eyes
4 oz. (113 g.) polyester fiberfill
  stuffing
Matching thread
6″ x 6″ (15 x 15 cm.) iron-on
  interfacing

PATTERN PIECES

BABY

1. COWL
2. BODY
3. HEAD GUSSET
4. BELLY GUSSET
5. ARM
6. LEG
7. FOOT

EGG

8. BOTTOM EGG
9. TOP EGG

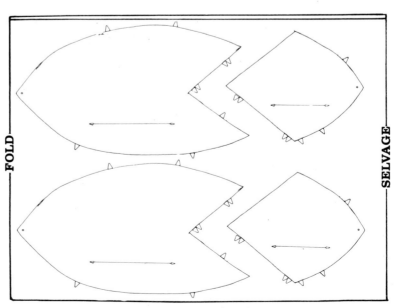

SELVAGE

FOLD

Main Color

SELVAGE

FOLD

Contrast Color

SEAM ALLOWANCE IS ¼″ (6 mm.)

FOLD

SELVAGE

Quilted Fabric/Lining

1.

- Right sides together, matching notches, pin together two arm pieces.
- Stitch from double notch to double notch. Leave opening between double notches.
- Clip curves. Turn arm right side out.
- Repeat for remaining arm pieces.

2.

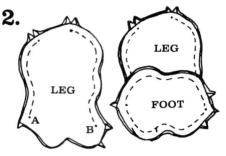

- Right sides together, matching notches and circles, pin together two leg pieces.
- Stitch from circle at A to double notch, and from circle at B to double notch. Leave opening between double notches.
- Right sides together, matching notches, pin foot to leg.
- Stitch, starting and stopping at circles.
- Clip curves. Turn leg right side out through double notches.
- Repeat for remaining leg and foot.

3.

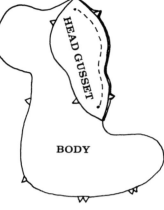

- Right sides together, matching notches, pin head gusset to left side of body. Baste. Stitch from circle to circle.
- Repeat for head gusset to right side of body.

4.

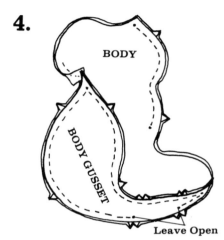

- Right sides together, matching notches, pin belly gusset to left side of body. Baste.
- Stitch from circle to circle. Leave opening between double notches.
- Repeat for belly gusset and right side of body. Do not leave opening between double notches.

5.

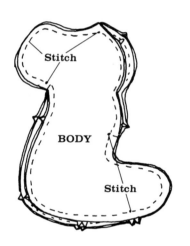

- Right sides together, matching notches, finish stitching remaining seams on body together as shown. Stitch from circle to circle. Clip curves. Turn right side out.

6.

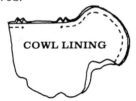

- Right sides together, matching notches, pin cowl together as shown.
- Stitch from A to B. Do not leave opening between double notches.
- Clip curves.
- Press.

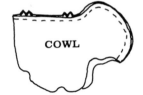

- Following manufacturer's instructions, press iron-on interfacing to cowl lining.
- Right sides together, matching notches, pin cowl lining together. Stitch as for cowl, except leave opening between double notches.
- Clip curves.
- Press.

7.

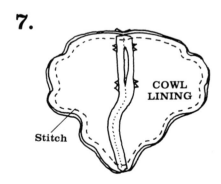

- Right sides together, matching outside edges, pin cowl lining to cowl.
- Stitch around outside of cowl as shown.
- Clip curves; trim seams.
- Turn right side out through opening in cowl lining.
- Slipstitch opening closed.
- Press.

- Apply eyes.

8.

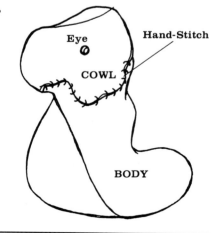

- Stuff arms.
- Stuff legs.
- Stuff body.
- Slipstitch all openings closed.
- Hand-stitch cowl to head as shown.

9.

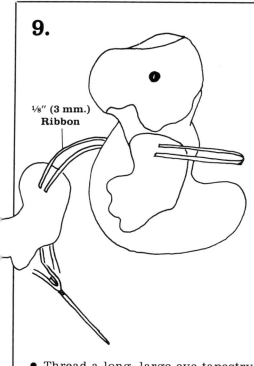

⅛″ (3 mm.) Ribbon

- Thread a long, large-eye tapestry needle with 24″ (60 cm.) of ⅛″ (3 mm.) ribbon.
- Push needle through arm at marks. Proceed through body at marks and continue through remaining arm. Go back through arm-body-arm. Holding both ends of ribbon, pull it snug and knot-tie a decorative bow.
- Repeat for attaching legs to body.

10.   THE EGG

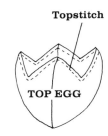

Stitch

BOTTOM EGG   TOP EGG

- Right sides together, matching notches, sequentially sew the four pieces of quilted fabric together. This will result in a spherical shape.
- Repeat for top of egg.
- Repeat for egg lining.
- Repeat for top of egg lining.

11.

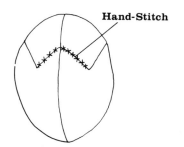

Leave Open

LINING   BOTTOM EGG

- Right sides together, matching notches, insert lining inside quilted egg. Pin.
- Choose one set of double notches to leave open for turning.
- Stitch from double notch to double notch.
- Trim and clip seams. Turn right side out through opening. Press. Turn under seam allowance between double notches, and baste closed.

12.

Topstitch

TOP EGG

- Topstitch along upper edge of egg.
- Repeat for top of egg.

13.

Hand-Stitch

- Hand-stitch top and bottom of egg together as shown.
- Insert baby into egg.

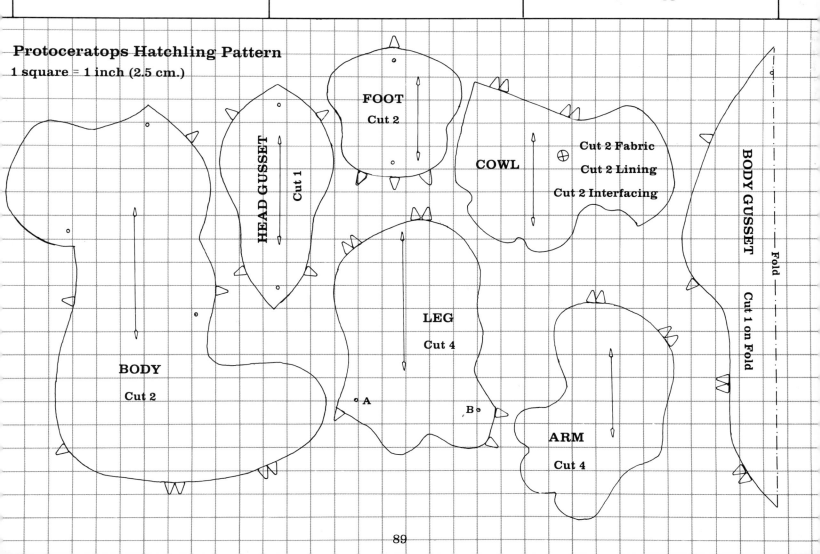

Protoceratops Hatchling Pattern
1 square = 1 inch (2.5 cm.)

FOOT Cut 2

HEAD GUSSET Cut 1

COWL Cut 2 Fabric Cut 2 Lining Cut 2 Interfacing

BODY GUSSET Cut 1 on Fold   Fold

LEG Cut 4

BODY Cut 2

A   B

ARM Cut 4

Protoceratops Hatchling Pattern

1 square = 1 inch (2.5 cm.)

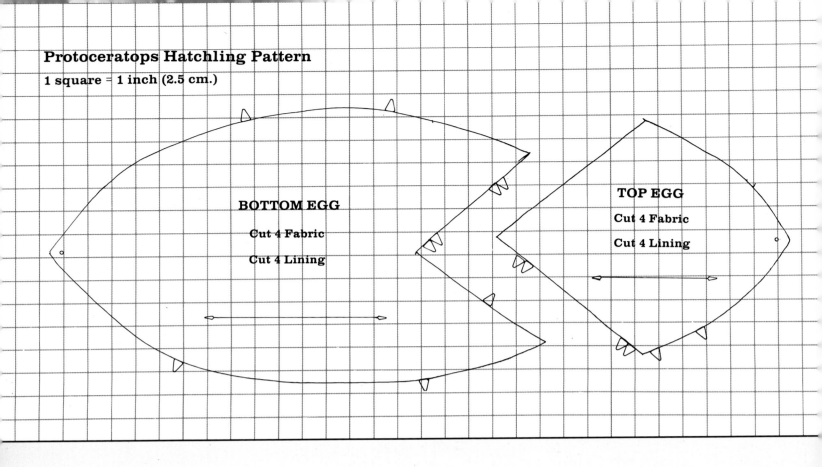

BOTTOM EGG

Cut 4 Fabric

Cut 4 Lining

TOP EGG

Cut 4 Fabric

Cut 4 Lining

Wind Toys

Ichthyosaurus

Ichthyosaurus Wind Sock

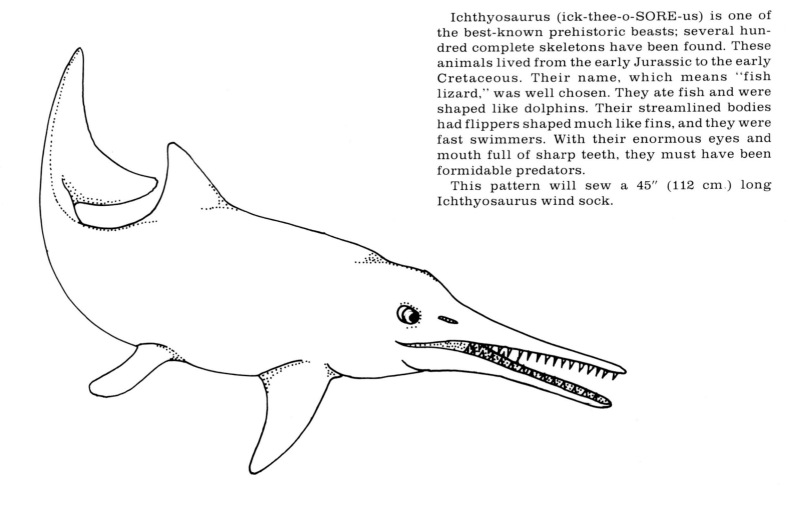

Ichthyosaurus (ick-thee-o-SORE-us) is one of the best-known prehistoric beasts; several hundred complete skeletons have been found. These animals lived from the early Jurassic to the early Cretaceous. Their name, which means "fish lizard," was well chosen. They ate fish and were shaped like dolphins. Their streamlined bodies had flippers shaped much like fins, and they were fast swimmers. With their enormous eyes and mouth full of sharp teeth, they must have been formidable predators.

This pattern will sew a 45″ (112 cm.) long Ichthyosaurus wind sock.

FABRIC REQUIREMENTS

This is a pattern that relies on surface design. The sample is silk fabric that has been painted with the watercolor technique. Other light-weight fabrics would also be acceptable. Just remember that a wind sock is very much like a kite: it needs to be light to fly properly.

45″ (112 cm.) fabric
Main fabric:
1 yd. (90 cm.)

NOTIONS

4″ (10 cm.) ring (plastic or wood). The bottom half of an embroidery hoop works well.
Matching thread
Small plastic ring for hanging
1 yd. (90 cm.) kite string

PATTERN PIECES

1. BODY
2. FRONT FIN
3. BACK FIN

SEAM ALLOWANCE IS ¼″ (6 mm.)

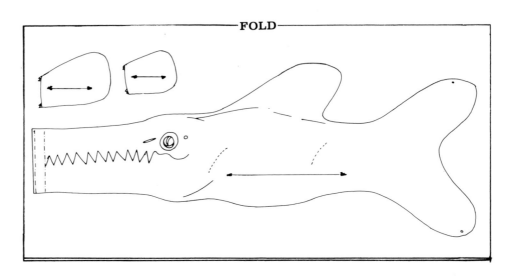

FOLD

1.

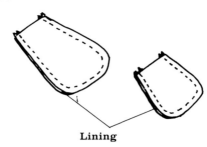

Lining

- Right sides together, matching outside edge, pin two front fin pieces together.
- Stitch around fin from double notch to double notch, as shown.
- Trim and clip seam.
- Turn front fin right side out.
- Turn under seam allowance, and baste opening closed.
- Repeat for remaining front fin.
- Repeat for back fins.

2.

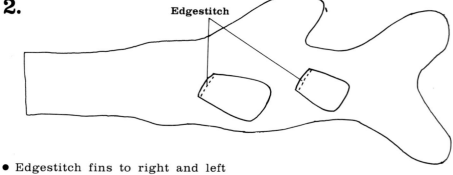

Edgestitch

- Edgestitch fins to right and left body halves where marked.

3.

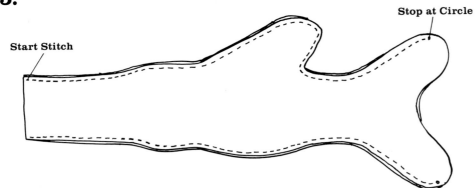

Start Stitch

Stop at Circle

- Right sides together, matching outside edges, pin right and left body pieces together. Leave openings at top and bottom as shown. Start and stop seam at circles.

- Trim and clip seams.
- Turn wind sock right side out.
- Press.

4.

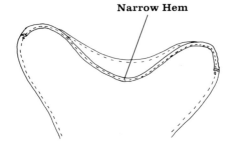

Narrow Hem

- Hem unfinished edge of tail with a narrow hem.

5.

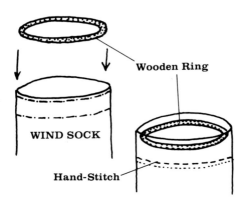

Wooden Ring

WIND SOCK

Hand-Stitch

- Turn under ¼" (6 mm.) of mouth casing to inside. Place ring inside of mouth and turn along fold line to cover. Hand-stitch casing to body.

6.

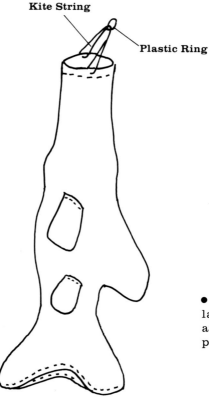

Kite String

Plastic Ring

- To hang wind sock, thread an extra-large needle with kite string, and attach it to the wooden ring and small plastic ring as shown.

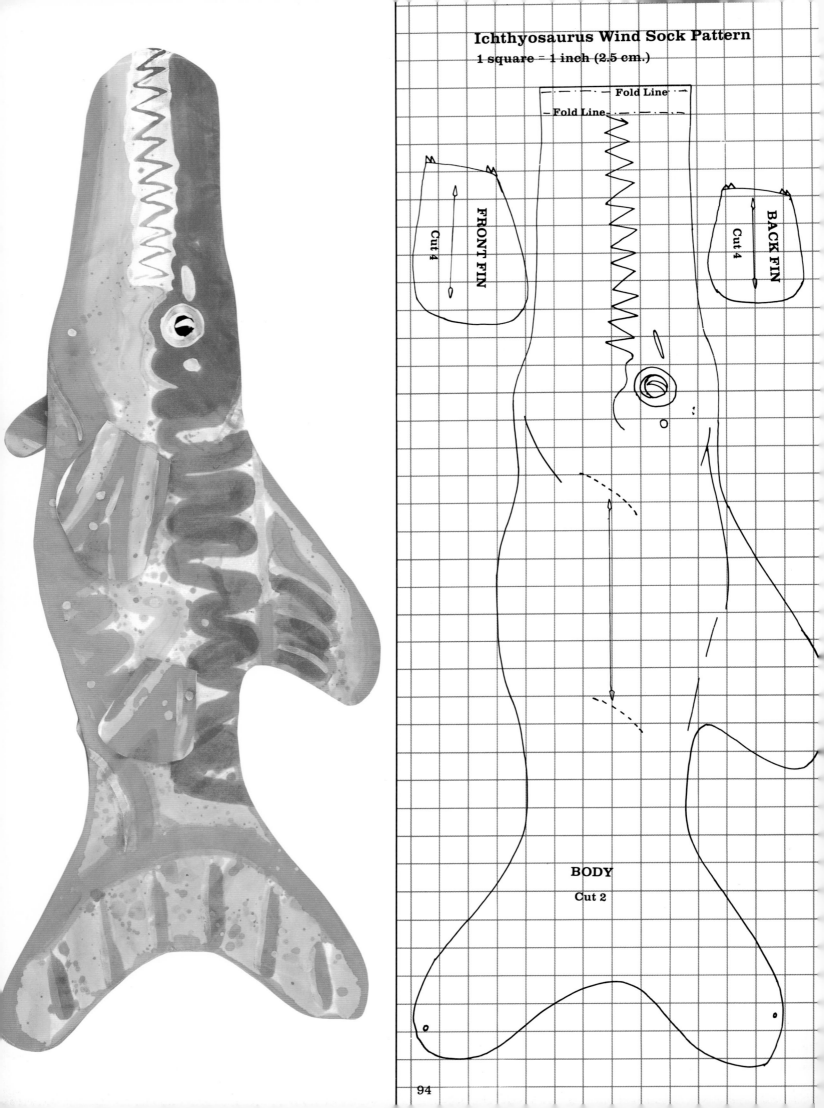

Ichthyosaurus Wind Sock Pattern
1 square = 1 inch (2.5 cm.)

Fold Line

Fold Line

FRONT FIN

Cut 4

BACK FIN

Cut 4

BODY

Cut 2

94

Quetzalcoatlus

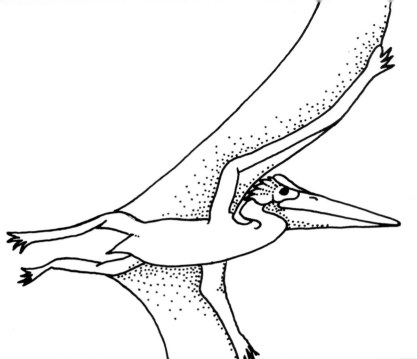

Quetzalcoatlus Delta Kite

This pterosaur, Quetzalcoatlus (ket-zal-ko-AAT-lus), had a wingspan of 40 feet (12 meters) and a body large enough to have looked many of the big dinosaurs in the eye. Yet it had an incredible ability to soar high above the ground. It is believed that when the sun warmed the earth to create a thermal updraft, this reptile jumped off the ground, flapped its powerful wings a few times, and took off. Riding thermal updrafts, it stayed in the air all day long, with very little expenditure of energy.

This pattern will sew a 60″ (150 cm.) delta kite.

Quetzalcoatlus Delta Kite Layout

FABRIC REQUIREMENTS

The sample for this kite was sewn from a unique nylon fabric called Tactel. Currently being manufactured for the sports industry, this modern fabric comes in lots of very bright colors. Lightweight and wind-resistant, it isn't slippery or difficult to sew. Alternatively, this kite could be made with a nylon fabric known as ripstop, which unfortunately is not nearly as easy to work with. The important qualities for kite fabric are light weight and a tight weave. This kite could also be sewn from silk or cotton broadcloth and painted with fabric paints. To add durability to your kite after it is appliquéd, use a fabric sealant on all seams.

60″ (150 cm.) fabric
Main color (yellow):
    1 yd. (90 cm.)
Green:
    ⅞ yd. (77 cm.)
Pink:
    ⅞ yd. (77 cm.)
Accent colors:
    ⅛ yd. (11 cm.) each
    Light purple
    Dark purple
    Blue

NOTIONS

Two 19 mm. safety eyes
Three 3/16″ (5 mm.) and one ¼″
    (6 mm.) wooden dowels, all 36″
    (90 cm.) long
Matching thread
Contrast thread
4″ (10 cm.) flexible plastic tubing
    ¼″ (6 mm.) I.D. (interior diameter)
1″ (2.5 cm.) of ¼″ (6 mm.) twill tape
Kite string
And when you are ready to fly your
    kite, of course, a light wind.

PATTERN PIECES

1. WING
2. BODY
3. FEET

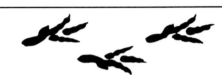

SEAM ALLOWANCE IS ¼″ (6 mm.)

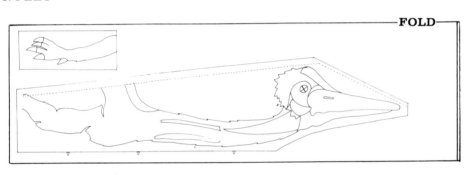

—FOLD—

SINGLE LAYER

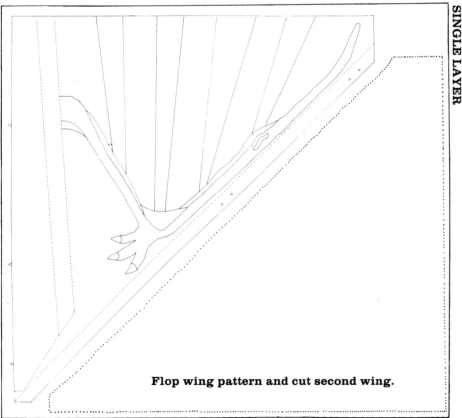

Flop wing pattern and cut second wing.

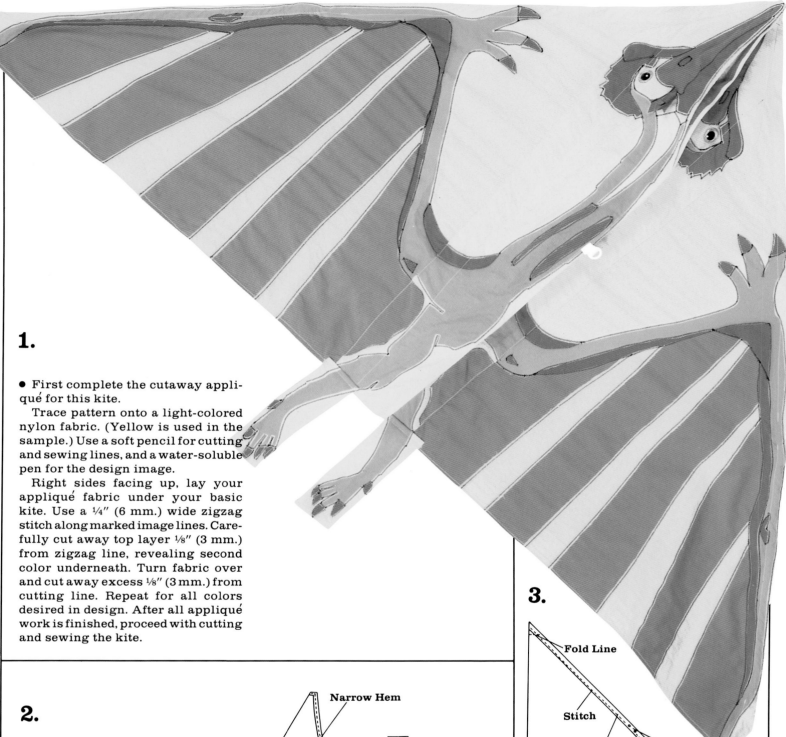

1.

- First complete the cutaway appliqué for this kite.

Trace pattern onto a light-colored nylon fabric. (Yellow is used in the sample.) Use a soft pencil for cutting and sewing lines, and a water-soluble pen for the design image.

Right sides facing up, lay your appliqué fabric under your basic kite. Use a ¼″ (6 mm.) wide zigzag stitch along marked image lines. Carefully cut away top layer ⅛″ (3 mm.) from zigzag line, revealing second color underneath. Turn fabric over and cut away excess ⅛″ (3 mm.) from cutting line. Repeat for all colors desired in design. After all appliqué work is finished, proceed with cutting and sewing the kite.

2.

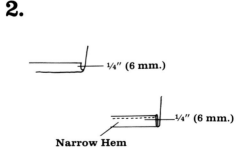

¼″ (6 mm.)

¼″ (6 mm.)

Narrow Hem

- Place all fabric pieces right side down.
- Turn ¼″ (6 mm.) over along edges marked for narrow hem, and press flat.
- Turn again ¼″ (6 mm.) and press flat.
- Pin or baste.
- Stitch along first turned edge, as shown.

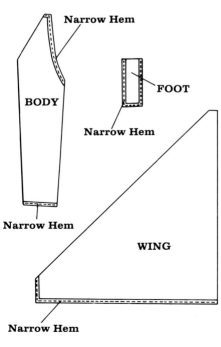

Narrow Hem

BODY

FOOT

Narrow Hem

Narrow Hem

WING

Narrow Hem

3.

Fold Line

Stitch

¾″ (19 mm.)

Circle

Dowel Pocket

- Place wings right side down.
- Turn over ¼″ (6 mm.) from diagonal edge and press flat.
- Turn again ¾″ (19 mm.) and press flat.
- Pin or baste.
- Stitch along first turned edge. Leave seam open between pairs of circle marks.
- Stitch bottom of pocket closed.
- Turn top of pocket down, along fold line, and stitch along turned edge.
- Repeat for remaining wing.

4.

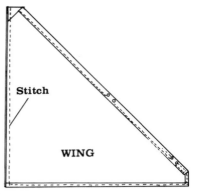

- Right sides together, matching notches, pin unfinished edge of wings together.
- Stitch together ¼″ (6 mm.) from edge.
- Press seam open.

5.

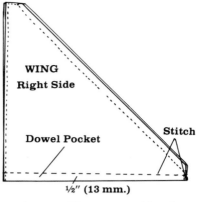

- Turn wings with wrong sides together, match edges, and press flat.
- Seam ½″ (13 mm.) from fold to form dowel pocket.
- Stitch top of dowel pocket closed.

6.

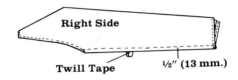

- Right sides together, matching notches, pin bodies together.
- Fold 1″ (2.5 cm.) of twill tape in half.
- Insert twill tape between bodies at x, matching unfinished edges; pin in place.
- Stitch ¼″ (6 mm.) from unfinished edge.
- Press seam open.

- Turn body with right sides out.
- Match edges and press flat.
- Stitch ½″ (13 mm.) from folded edge.

8.

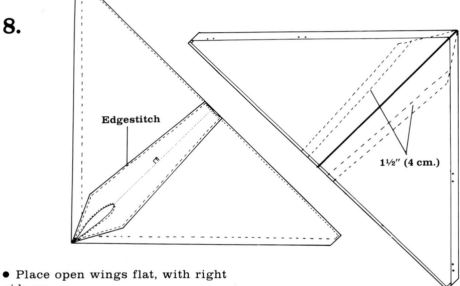

- Place open wings flat, with right side up.
- Match body, with right side up, to sewing lines on wings. Pin and baste body to wing.
- Edgestitch along turned, folded body edge.

- Turn kite over, right side down.
- Baste or pin body to wing 1½″ (4 cm.) from first stitched line.
- Stitch as shown.

7.

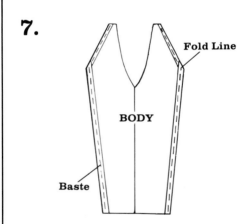

- Turn edges to wrong side along fold lines, and press turned edges flat.

9.

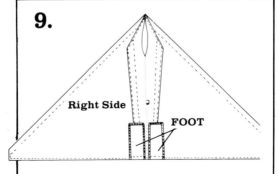

- Matching circles, place right side of foot to right side of body.
- Stitch ¼″ (6 mm.) from edge as shown.
- Press leg open, and seam again at turned edge.
- Repeat for remaining foot.
- Apply eyes.

10.

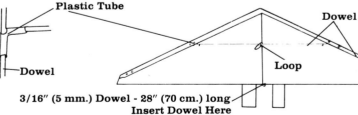

3/16″ (5 mm.) Dowel - 28″ (70 cm.) long
Insert Dowel Here

- Cut plastic tube in half to form two pieces, each 2″ (5 cm.) long.
- Cut a slit in center of tube, and bend.
- Cut two 3/16″ (5 mm.) dowels to 28″ (70 cm.) length.
- Insert 28″ (70 cm.) dowel in lower opening of wing pocket to center opening.
- Slip plastic tube on dowel and slide dowel in place.

- Repeat for other side of wing.
- Cut one 3/16″ (5 mm.) dowel to 31″ (78 cm.) in length.
- Insert in center dowel pocket, and hand-stitch opening closed.
- Lay kite flat on table and mark ¼″ (6 mm.) dowel to fit tightly between plastic tubes; cut and insert.
- Hand-sew loop to hold ¼″ (6 mm.) spreader dowel in place.
- Attach kite string to twill tape.

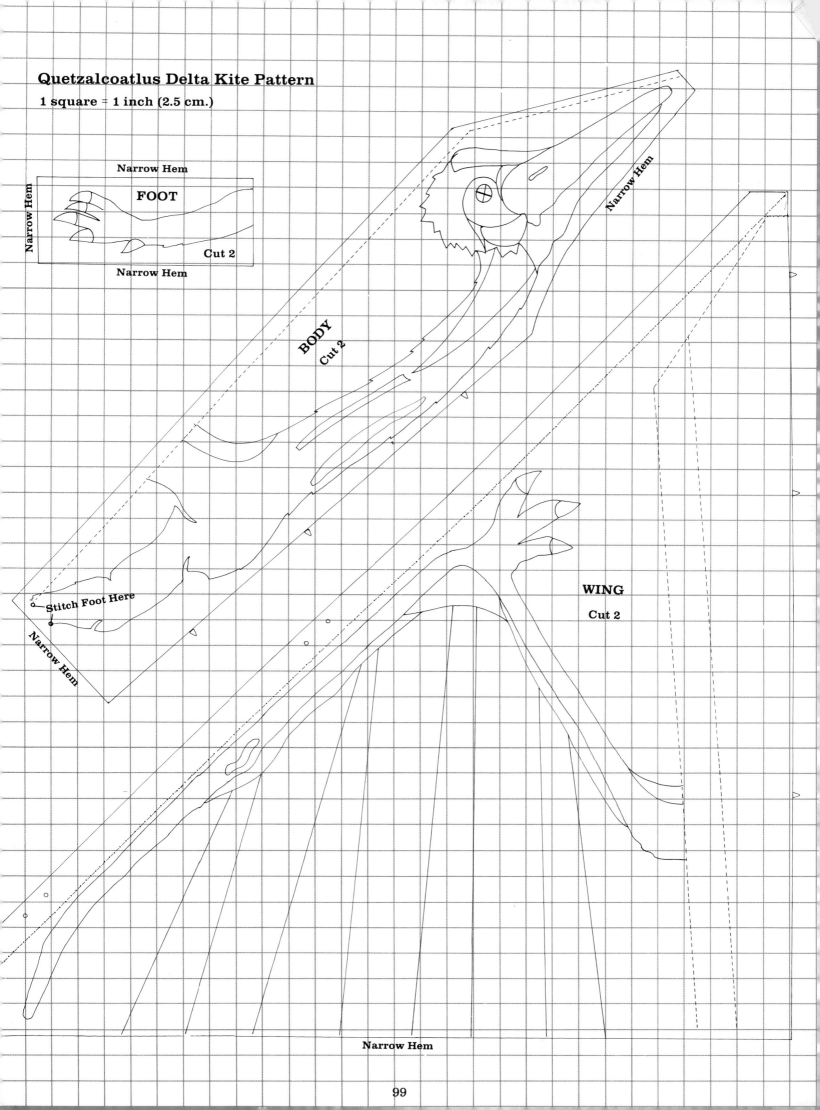

Quetzalcoatlus Delta Kite Pattern
1 square = 1 inch (2.5 cm.)

Narrow Hem

FOOT

Cut 2

Narrow Hem

Narrow Hem

Narrow Hem

Narrow Hem

BODY

Cut 2

WING

Cut 2

Stitch Foot Here

Narrow Hem

Narrow Hem

Rhamphorhynchus

Rhamphorhynchus Sled Kite

Rhamphorhynchus (ram-for-INK-us) was a small pterosaur with a slim, lightweight body, long wings, and a small head. This pterosaur had forward-pointing teeth that were probably used for spearing fish, and a long tail with a balancing rudder that was used for steering.

This pattern will sew a 24″ (60 cm.) tall Rhamphorhynchus sled kite.

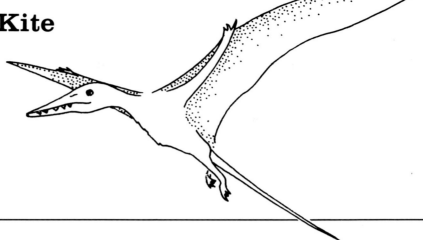

FABRIC REQUIREMENTS

The model that was photographed for this book was sewn from China silk, and the surface design was applied using silk paints. Alternatively, the same technique that was used for the Quetzalcoatlus delta kite would be successful for this one.

45″ (112 cm.) fabric
Main color:
    1½ yds. (135 cm.)

NOTIONS

6″ (15 cm.) twill tape ¼″ (6 mm.) wide
Three 24″ (60 cm.) wooden dowels
    ¼″ (6 mm.) in diameter
Small plastic ring
Kite string
Matching thread

SEAM ALLOWANCE IS ¼″ (6 mm.)

PATTERN PIECES

1. BODY
2. WING
3. SIDE WING
4. TAIL

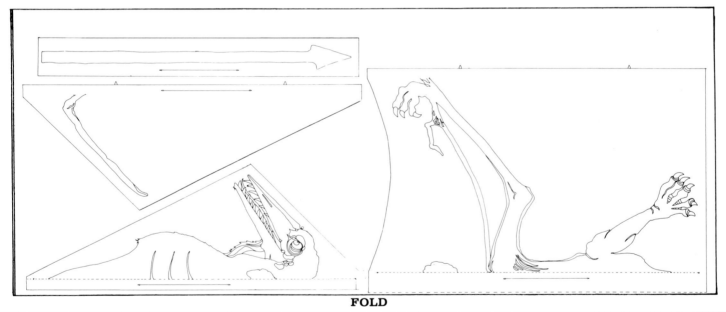

FOLD

1.

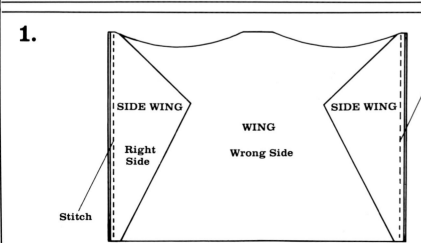

- Wrong sides facing, pin right and left side wings to wing. Stitch ¼″ (6 mm.) from edge as shown.
- Trim seam 1/16″ (1½ mm) from cut edge.
- Press seam open.

2.

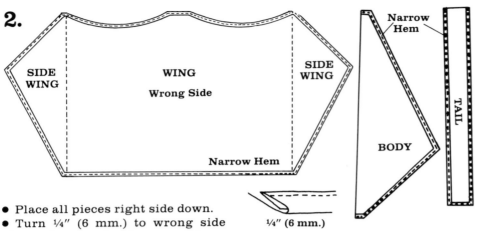

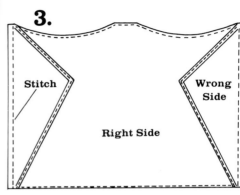

3.

- Place all pieces right side down.
- Turn ¼″ (6 mm.) to wrong side along edges marked for narrow hem, and press flat. Note: Curved area along top of wings should be clipped to lie flat.

¼″ (6 mm.)

- Turn ¼″ (6 mm.) again and press flat.
- Edgestitch along inside folded edge.

- Fold along stitching line that joins the wing and side wing, right sides together. This will encase the un-finished seam.
- Press. Pin.
- Stitch ½″ (13 mm.) from folded edge as shown. This will form the side dowel pockets.

4.

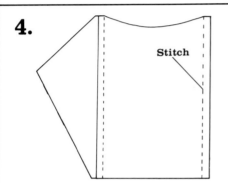

- Right sides together, fold wing assembly in half along center line.
- Press along fold. Pin.
- Seam with ½″ (13 mm.) allowance from fold line.

5.

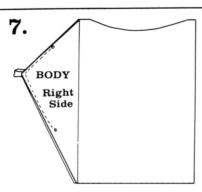

- Right sides facing down, place body on wing (right side facing up), match-ing the A line on wing to the A line on the body.

- Pin body to wing and stitch along marked line.
- Fold cut edge of body under ¼″ (6 mm.) and topstitch in place on wing.
- Repeat for other side of body.

6.

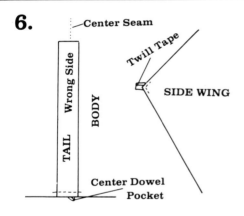

- Right sides together, matching circles, place tail along center line of kite.
- Seam ¼″ (6 mm.) from unfinished edge on tail.
- Unfold tail to cover new edge, and press flat.
- Topstitch along turned edge.

- Fold 2″ (5 cm.) piece of twill tape in half and pin to wrong side of side wing tip.
- Stitch securely through wing tip and twill tape.
- Repeat for other side wing tip.

7.

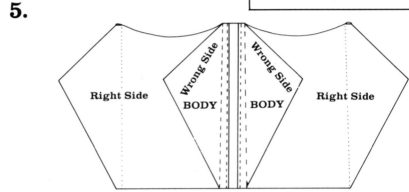

- Fold 2″ (5 cm.) piece of twill tape in half.
- Place between body halves as shown.
- Pin and baste securely in place.
- Seam body halves together from circle to circle.

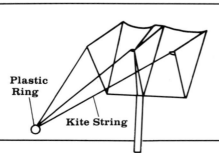

Plastic Ring

Kite String

8.

- Insert dowels cut to 24″ (60 cm.) into all three dowel pockets. Hand-stitch openings closed.
- Tie three 65″ (163 cm.) lengths of kite string to twill tape loops. Grasp the three lengths together and tie to small plastic ring, making sure that the lengths of string are equal.

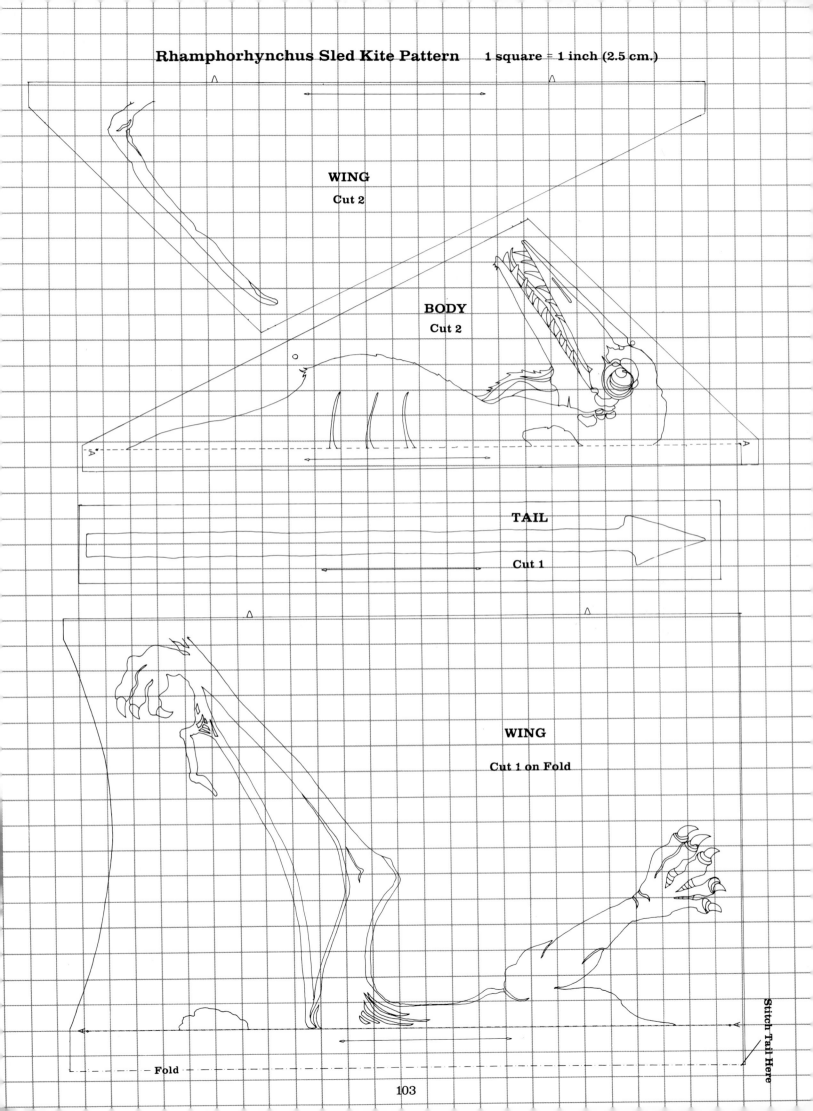

Rhamphorhynchus Sled Kite Pattern   1 square = 1 inch (2.5 cm.)

WING

Cut 2

BODY

Cut 2

TAIL

Cut 1

WING

Cut 1 on Fold

Stitch Tail Here

Fold

Puppets

Hadrosaurs

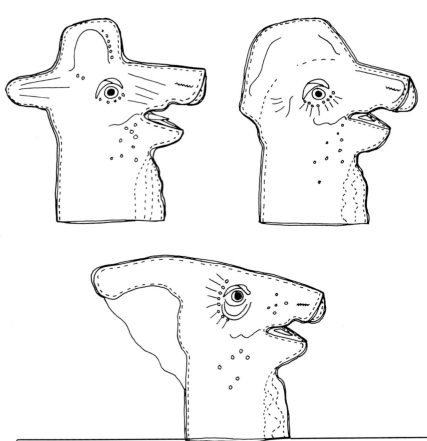

Hadrosaurs

Hadrosaurs (HAD-ro-sores) were duck-billed dinosaurs, the most diverse and abundant type in late Cretaceous North America. All hadrosaurs had heavy bodies and long heads with broad, flat, horny bills, but they varied greatly in the way the tops of their heads developed. Hadrosaurs are best known for their crests (even though not all Hadrosaurs were crested).

Lambeosaurus (lam-bee-o-SORE-us) was the first crested hadrosaur found in North America. His crest was hatchet-shaped and, like other Hadrosaurs, he was a vegetarian.

Hypacrosaurus (hi-pak-ro-SORE-us) lived during the middle of the late Cretaceous period. This large duckbill had a sizable hollow crest on its head.

Parasaurolophus (par-a-sore-o-LO-fus) lived to the end of the Cretaceous period, longer than any other Hadrosaurs. They were 30 feet (nine meters) long with hoofed toes, short forelimbs, and webbed fingers.

This pattern will sew 11″ (28 cm.) high puppet heads of Lambeosaurus, Hypacrosaurus, and Parasaurolophus.

Hadrosaur Puppets Layout

FABRIC REQUIREMENTS

Felt is the best fabric for these patterns; any color will do. If you decide not to use felt, you will have to add a seam allowance to the patterns.

The detail in these puppets was painted using shiny dimensional fabric paint. Because this kind of paint drags on a sewing machine and gums up the needle, in this case I recommend sewing these puppets and then applying the paint.

Fabric amounts are for three puppets.

72″ (180 cm.) fabric

Main color:
½ yd. (45 cm.)

Tongue color:
5″ x 5″ (13 by 13 cm.)

Gusset color:
10″ x 10″ (25 by 25 cm.)

Parasaurolophus skin flap:
5″ x 10″ (13 by 25 cm.)

NOTIONS
(for three puppets)

Six 19 mm. safety eyes
Matching thread

Optional

Squeaker

PATTERN PIECES

1. HEAD
2. EYELID
3. MOUTH
4. TONGUE
5. SKIN FLAP (Parasaurolophus)

SEAM ALLOWANCE IS ⅛″ (3 cm.)

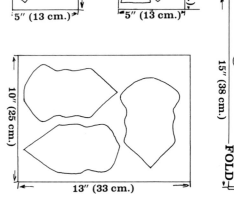

10″ (25 cm.)

5″ (13 cm.)

5″ (13 cm.)

5″ (13 cm.)

10″ (25 cm.)

13″ (33 cm.)

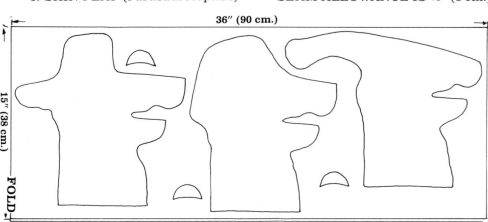

36″ (90 cm.)

15″ (38 cm.)

FOLD

1.

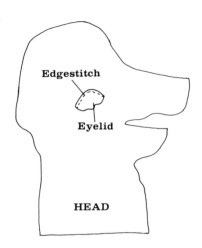

- Right sides facing out, pin eyelid to marks on head. Edgestitch eyelid to head as shown.
- Repeat for remaining side of head and eyelid.

2.

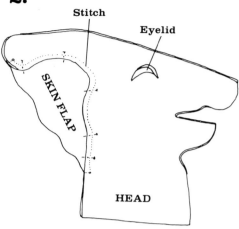

PARASAUROLOPHUS ONLY

- Pin skin flap between head pieces as shown.

3.

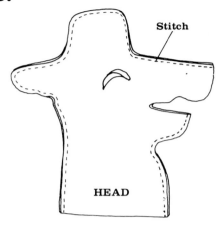

- Right sides facing out, matching shapes, place head pieces together.
- Pin and stitch ⅛″ (3 mm.) from cut edge as shown.

4.

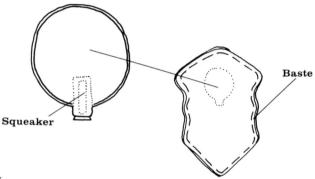

OPTIONAL

To install a squeaker in the mouth:
- Cut two mouth pieces from felt.

- Baste pieces together after inserting a squeaker into the upper section of the mouth.

5.

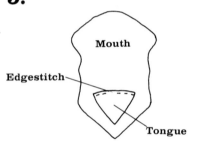

- Right sides facing out, pin tongue to mark on mouth. Edgestitch tongue to mouth as shown.

6.

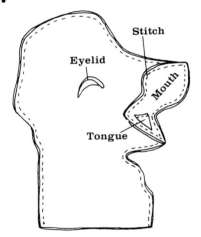

- Right sides facing out, matching shapes, fit mouth to head pieces. Pin and stitch ⅛″ (3 mm.) from cut edge.

7.

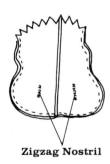

- Use a small zigzag stitch to quilt the nostrils.

8.

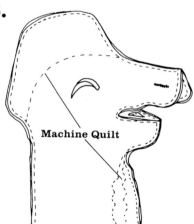

- Machine quilt remaining details as indicated on individual puppet patterns.

- Apply eyes.

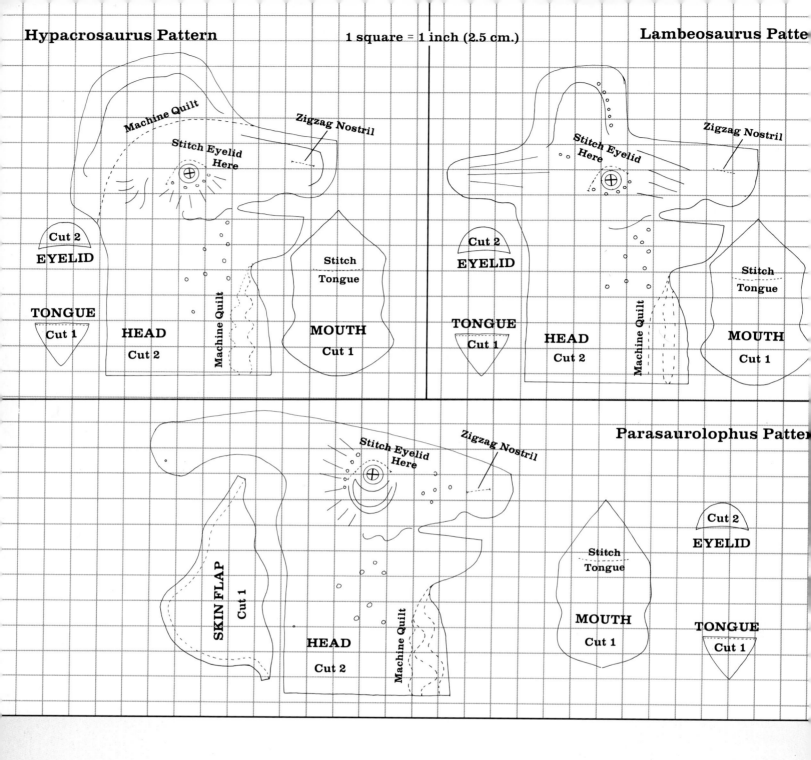

Hypacrosaurus Pattern

1 square = 1 inch (2.5 cm.)

Lambeosaurus Pattern

Machine Quilt

Stitch Eyelid Here

Zigzag Nostril

Cut 2

EYELID

Stitch Tongue

TONGUE

Cut 1

HEAD

Cut 2

Machine Quilt

MOUTH

Cut 1

Stitch Eyelid Here

Zigzag Nostril

Cut 2

EYELID

Stitch Tongue

TONGUE

Cut 1

HEAD

Cut 2

Machine Quilt

MOUTH

Cut 1

Parasaurolophus Pattern

Stitch Eyelid Here

Zigzag Nostril

SKIN FLAP

Cut 1

HEAD

Cut 2

Machine Quilt

Cut 2

EYELID

Stitch Tongue

MOUTH

Cut 1

TONGUE

Cut 1

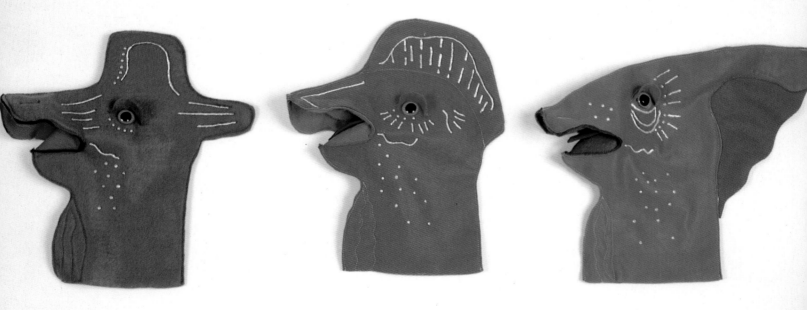

Allosaurus

Wearables

Allosaurus Appliqué for Sweatshirt

Allosaurus (al-o-SORE-us) was a meat-eating dinosaur that lived in North America during the late Jurassic period. It had a distinctive skull with a ridge along the top that ran from between the eyes to the tip of the snout. There were also bumps above the eyes. This image of Allosaurus makes children laugh as they lift up his mouth to show his tongue and teeth. For some added fun, slip a squeaker into the top of the mouth before appliquéing the image to a sweatshirt.

This appliqué pattern will fit a wide variety of sizes.

FABRIC REQUIREMENTS

The sample shirt pictured was done with machine appliqué, a good choice for a garment to be worn by a child, because it will stand up to lots of machine washing and lots of fun. This appliqué is made up of lots of different colors and textures of fabric. If you don't want to use the accent colors as illustrated, you could just let the basic Allosaurus shape stand alone.

45″ (112 cm.) fabric
Main color:
    ½ yd. (45 cm.)

NOTIONS

1 purchased sweatshirt or pattern and material for sweatshirt
Two buttons
16″ (40 cm.) of ½″ (13 mm.) jumbo rickrack
Matching thread
Contrasting thread

PATTERN PIECES

1. BODY
2. HEAD
3. TONGUE

SEAM ALLOWANCE IS ¼″ (6 mm.)

1.

• Appliqué all details onto body and head pieces.

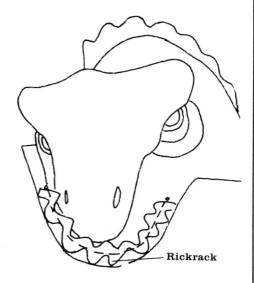

Rickrack

• Baste rickrack to head as shown, starting and stopping at circles.

2.

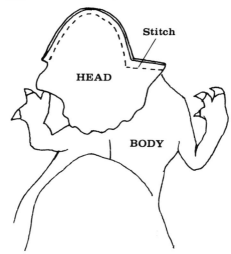

Stitch

HEAD

BODY

• Right sides together, pin head to body as shown.
• Stitch.
• Clip seam and turn head right side out.

3.

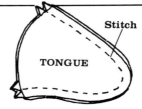

Stitch

TONGUE

• Right sides together, pin tongue pieces together.
• Stitch as shown. Trim seam and turn tongue right side out.

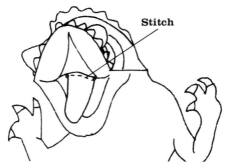

Stitch

• Turn under seam allowance on tongue and stitch to mouth between circles, as shown.

4.

- Appliqué design onto shirt.
- You can appliqué the design onto a purchased sweatshirt or use a commercial pattern to sew a sweatshirt. There are many simple and easy-to-sew sweatshirt patterns available. It is more difficult to appliqué this design onto a purchased sweatshirt because the Allosaurus is a complex design requiring lots of changes of direction as you sew. A purchased sweatshirt cannot be laid flat and so is difficult to maneuver on the sewing machine. If you are sewing from a commercial pattern, appliqué the design onto the front and back after sewing the side seam as shown.

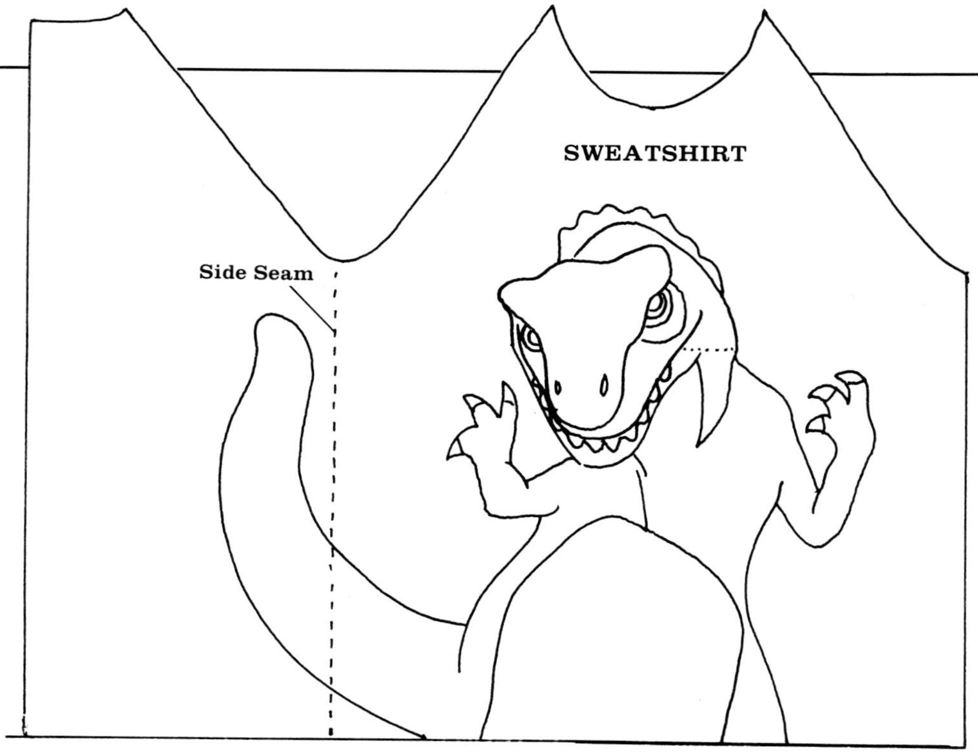

SWEATSHIRT

Side Seam

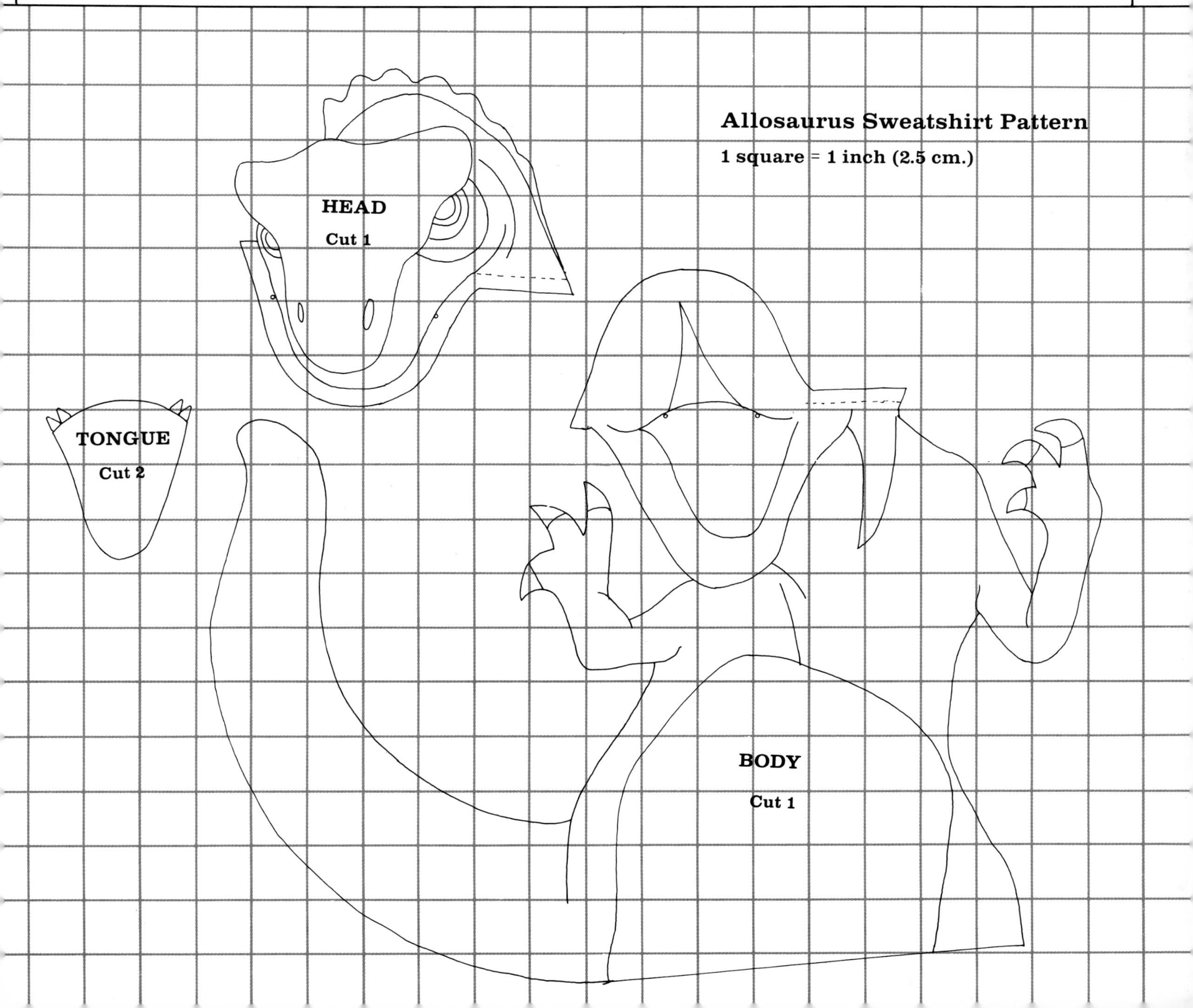

Allosaurus Sweatshirt Pattern

1 square = 1 inch (2.5 cm.)

HEAD
Cut 1

TONGUE
Cut 2

BODY
Cut 1

Allosaurus Appliqué for Sweatshirt

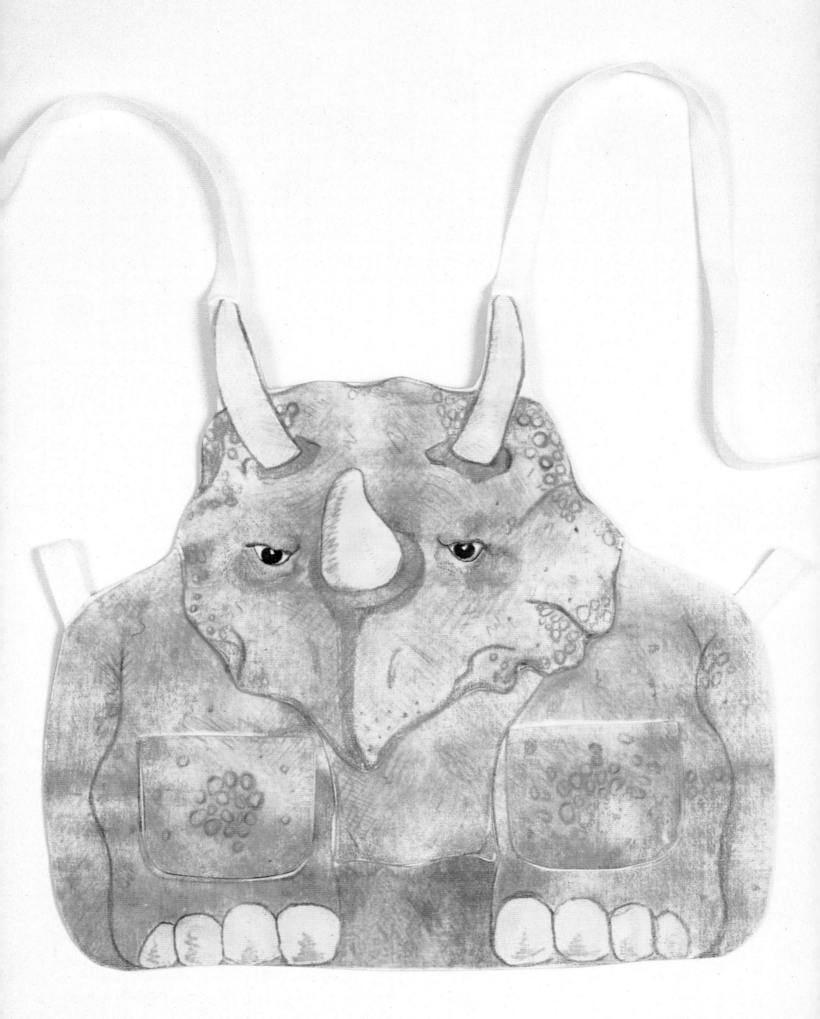

Triceratops Apron

Triceratops Apron

Triceratops is one of my favorite dinosaurs, perhaps because it's the first one I ever sewed. This apron uses Triceratops' horns and square shape to create a wearable-art apron.

This pattern will sew an apron to fit children from ages 2 to 10.

FABRIC REQUIREMENTS

This pattern relies on surface design. Without the image of Triceratops drawn, painted, or needleworked on the fabric, this apron is merely an ordinary one. The sample for this book was drawn with transfer crayons. I used a lightweight canvas for the apron and lined it with a lightweight cotton fabric.

45″ (112 cm.) fabric

Main color:
¾ yd. (68 cm.)

Lining:
¾ yd. (68 cm.)

NOTIONS

Matching thread
64″ (160 cm.) of ½″ (13 mm.) webbing or grosgrain ribbon

OPTIONAL

Squeaker

SEAM ALLOWANCE IS ½″ (13 mm.)

PATTERN PIECES

1. HEAD
2. BODY
3. KNEE POCKET
4. BELLY POCKET

LAYOUT

Use same layout for fabric and lining.

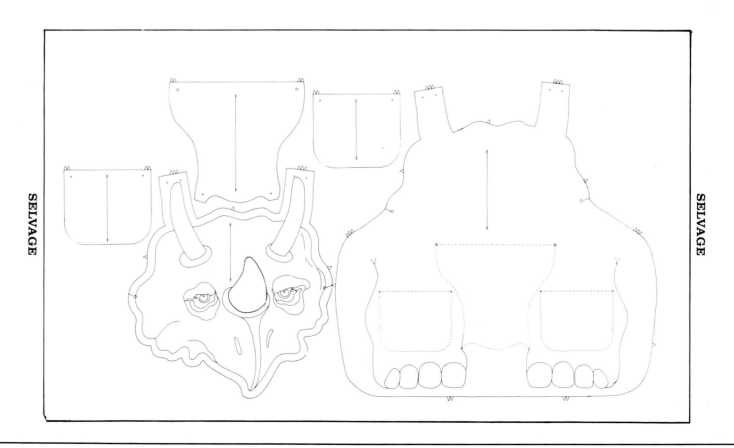

SELVAGE

SELVAGE

1.

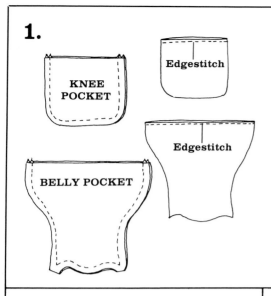

KNEE POCKET

Edgestitch

Edgestitch

BELLY POCKET

- Right sides together, matching notches, pin knee pocket to knee pocket lining.
- Stitch; leave opening between double notches.
- Clip curves, and turn right side out through opening.
- Press.
- Turn ¼″ (6 mm.) seam allowance between double notches to inside. Pin and baste.
- Edgestitch opening closed.
- Repeat for remaining knee pocket and lining.
- Repeat for belly pocket and lining.

2.

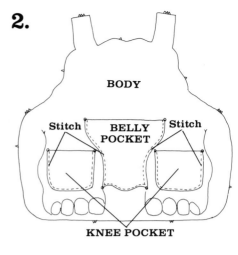

BODY

Stitch   BELLY POCKET   Stitch

KNEE POCKET

- Matching stitching lines and circles, pin the pockets in place on the body of Triceratops.
- Edgestitch pockets in place. Don't forget to securely backstitch at beginning and end of seam.

3.

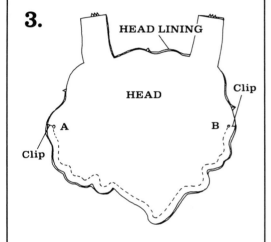

HEAD LINING

HEAD

Clip

A   B

Clip

- Right sides together, matching notches, pin head to head lining.
- Stitch from A to B.
- Clip curves between A and B. Clip at A and B.
- Turn head and press.

4.

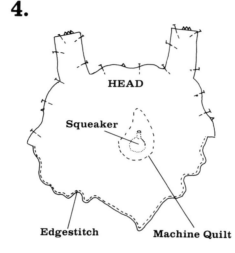

HEAD

Squeaker

Edgestitch   Machine Quilt

- Edgestitch head from A to B. Pin loose lining to fabric as shown.

OPTIONAL

- Machine quilt along marked lines on nose horn. Before finishing sewing the horn seam, slip a squeaker into pocket that is being formed between fabric and lining. Finish seam.

5.

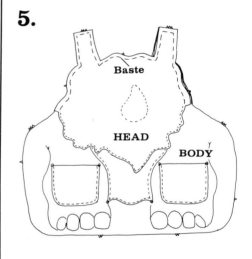

Baste

HEAD

BODY

- Match head to body, right sides facing out.
- Pin head in place on body. Baste through all layers.

6.

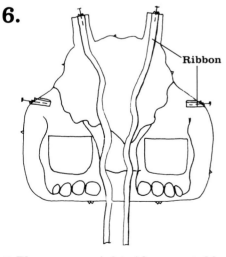

Ribbon

- Place apron right side up on table.
- Cut ribbon into two 29″ (73 cm.) pieces and pin at horns (triple notches). Cut remaining ribbon into two 7″ (18 cm.) pieces. Fold these pieces in half and pin at shoulders (triple notches).

7.

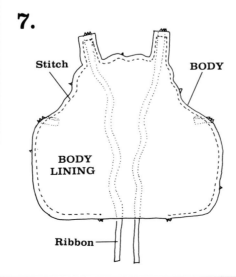

Stitch   BODY

BODY LINING

Ribbon

- Take care to avoid catching loose ends of ribbons in seam.
- Right sides together, matching notches, pin lining to apron.
- Stitch seam. Leave opening between double notches.
- Clip curves and trim seams.
- Turn apron right side out through opening.
- Press.
- Turn under seam allowance at opening. Pin and baste closed.
- Edgestitch around outside of apron.
- To wear, thread ribbons through diagonally opposite loops.

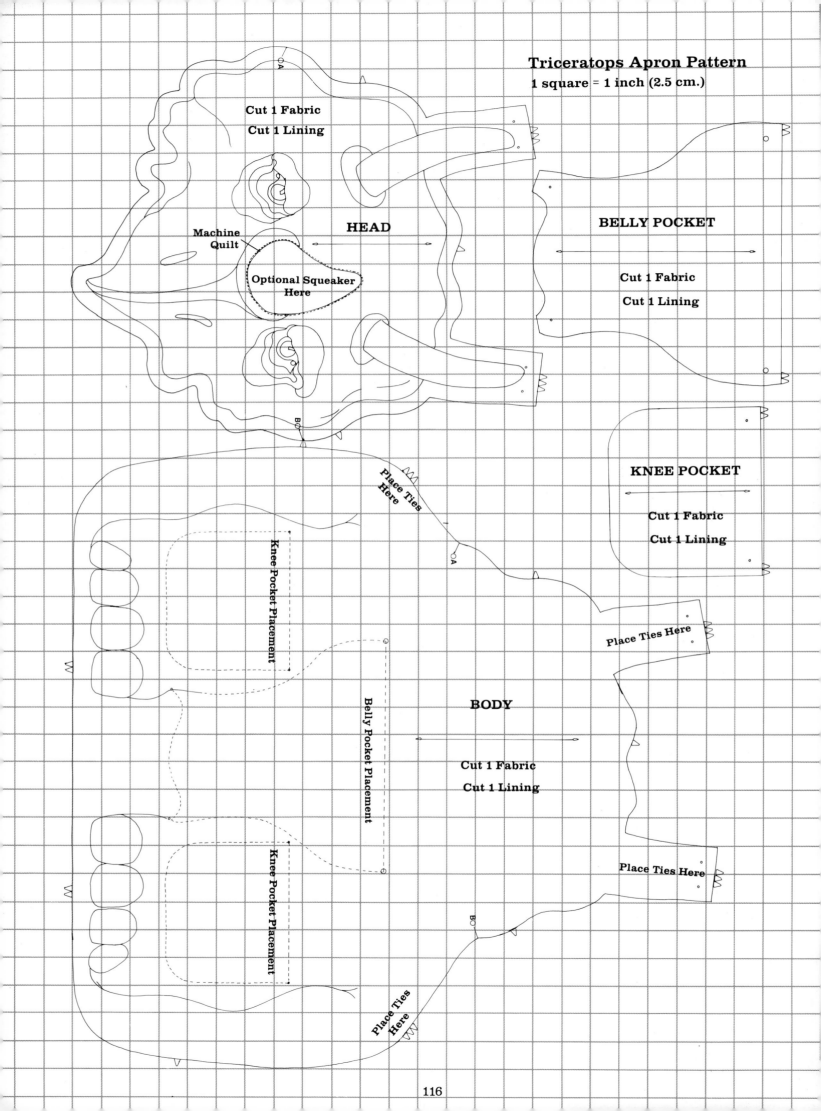

Triceratops Apron Pattern
1 square = 1 inch (2.5 cm.)

Cut 1 Fabric

Cut 1 Lining

HEAD

BELLY POCKET

Machine
Quilt

Optional Squeaker
Here

Cut 1 Fabric

Cut 1 Lining

KNEE POCKET

Cut 1 Fabric

Cut 1 Lining

Place Ties
Here

Knee Pocket Placement

Belly Pocket Placement

Place Ties Here

BODY

Cut 1 Fabric

Cut 1 Lining

Knee Pocket Placement

Place Ties Here

Place Ties
Here

116

Triceratops Costume

To a child, a costume is a way to enter into a world of fantasy and play. A costume is dress-up, a play, a holiday, a chance to be someone or something different from the everyday.

Triceratops was a member of a class of dinosaurs called Ceratopsian. The Ceratopsian head pieces evolved from a simple helmet designed to protect the skull and neck into many different combinations of horns and frills. Although the variation of frill and horn was enormous, basically the helmet helped the animal to protect itself and fight its enemies.

This pattern will sew a Triceratops costume consisting of a helmet mask and a separate body costume.

HELMET MASK

The helmet mask will fit all children sizes and some adults.

FABRIC REQUIREMENTS

Cotton-poly broadcloth works well for the body and the helmet, and silver lamé fabric for the horns increases visibility at night. Whatever fabric you choose, keep in mind that a lightweight costume can always have a sweater worn with it, but a bulky one on an unexpectedly mild day can be very unpleasant for a child.

45″ (112 cm.) fabric
Main color:
   1 yd. (90 cm.)
Lining color:
   1¼ yd. (113 cm.)
Horn color:
   ¼ yd. (23 cm.)

NOTIONS

½″ (13 mm.) foam sheeting: 36″ x 36″ (90 x 90 cm.)
Felt scraps
Matching thread
Contrasting thread

PATTERN PIECES

1. COWL
2. HEAD
3. UPPER MOUTH
4. LOWER JAW
5. LOWER MOUTH
6. EYE
7. EYELID
8. FELT EYEBALL 1
9. FELT EYEBALL 2
10. SHORT HORN
11. LONG HORN

SEAM ALLOWANCE IS ½″ (13 mm.)

BODY COSTUME

FABRIC REQUIREMENTS

45″ (112 cm.) fabric
Main color:
   Small
      2¼ yds. (203 cm.)
   Medium & Large
      2½ yds. (225 cm.)
Lining color:
   Small
      1¼ yds. (113 cm.)
   Medium & Large
      1½ yds. (135 cm.)
Contrast color:
   Small & Medium
      ¾ yd. (68 cm.)
   Large
      1 yd. (90 cm.)
Knit ribbing:
   ¼ yd. (23 cm.)

PATTERN PIECES

1. FRONT
2. BACK BAND
3. BACK
4. SLEEVE
5. TAIL GUSSET
6. TAIL
7. TAIL CIRCLE
8. HAND

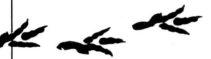

SEAM ALLOWANCE IS ⅝″ (15 mm.)

NOTIONS

½″ foam sheeting:
   36″ x 54″ (90 x 135 cm.): med./lg.
   36″ x 44″ (90 x 110 cm.): small
Matching thread
Contrasting thread
½″ (13 mm.) elastic:
   10″ (25 cm.)
Sizes small and medium:
   16″ (40 cm.) zipper
Size large:
   20″ (50 cm.) zipper
1 packet double-fold bias tape

SIZING

The body pattern will fit children:
Small:
   sizes 4-6; chest 23″-25″ (58-63 cm.)
Medium:
   sizes 6-8; chest 26″-27″ (65-68 cm.)
Large:
   sizes 10-12; chest 28″-30″ (70-75 cm.)

Contrast Color Body

FOLD

Main Color, Body
*Unfold - Cut 1

Helmet Fabric & Lining

*Unfold - Cut 1   FOLD

Horns, Fabric & Lining

FOLD

*Unfold - Cut 1

Foam Helmet

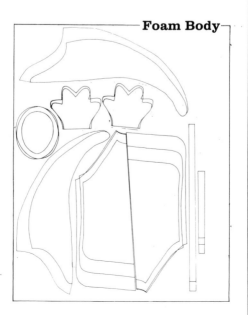

Foam Body

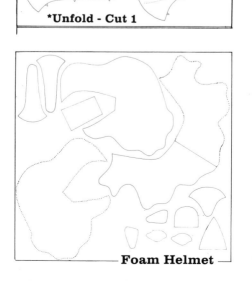

1.

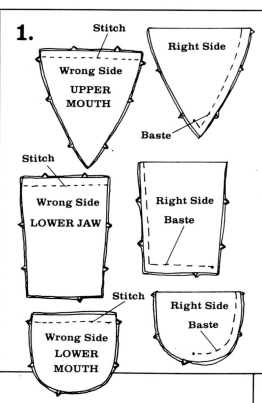

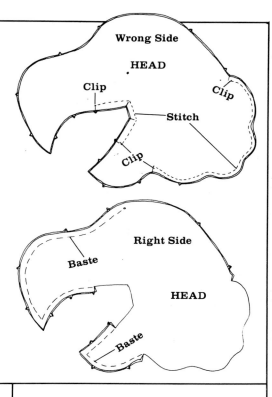

- Right sides together, matching notches, pin upper mouth lining and upper mouth together.
- Stitch as shown.
- Clip seams.
- Turn upper mouth right side out.
- Press.
- With right sides now out, pin loose edges of upper mouth lining and upper mouth together.
- Baste upper mouth and upper mouth lining together.

Repeat for:
- right head and right head lining.
- left head and left head lining.
- lower jaw and lower jaw lining.
- lower mouth and lower mouth lining.

2.

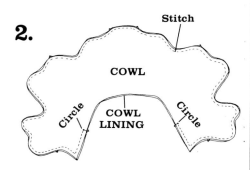

- Right sides together, matching notches, pin cowl lining to cowl.
- Stitch as shown.
- Clip.
- Turn cowl right side out through opening.

3.

COWL

Insert Foam

- Insert matching cowl foam piece into cowl fabric casing opening.
- Turn under seam allowance and baste opening closed.

4.

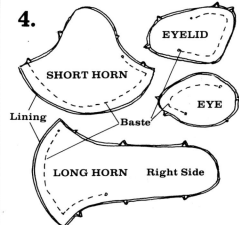

- Wrong sides together, matching notches, pin eye and eye lining together.
- Baste as shown.

Repeat for:
- remaining eye.
- eyelids.
- long horns.
- short horn.

5.

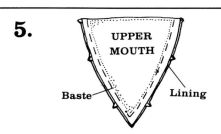

- Insert matching foam piece into upper mouth fabric casing opening.
- Pin remaining open seams together, encasing upper mouth foam between upper mouth and upper mouth lining.
- Baste remaining open seams closed. (This will finish encasing foam in fabric.)

Repeat for:
- right head.
- left head.
- lower jaw.
- lower mouth.
- eyes.
- eyelids.
- long horns.
- short horn.

6.

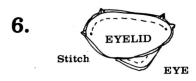

- Right sides together, matching notches, pin eye to eyelid along notched edges.
- Stitch as shown, starting and stopping at circles.
- Turn eye assembly right side out.
- Repeat for remaining eye and eyelid.

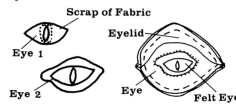

- Glue scrap of fabric (pupil) behind eye 1.
- Glue eye 1 to eye 2.
- Glue entire felt eye to marks on eye.
- Repeat for remaining eyeball and felt eye.

7.

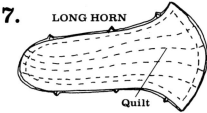

- Machine quilt along marked lines on long horn. Stitch through fabric, foam, and lining.

Repeat for:
- remaining long horn.
- cowl.
- short horn.
- right and left head.

8.

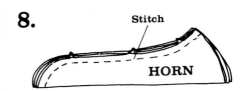

Stitch

HORN

- Right sides together, fold horns in half, and pin as shown.
- Stitch.
- Clip and trim seam.
- Turn horns right side out.

Repeat for:
- remaining long horn.
- short horn.

9.

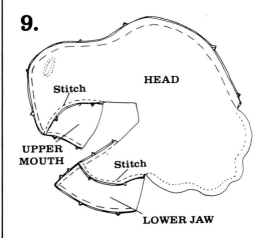

HEAD

Stitch

UPPER MOUTH

Stitch

LOWER JAW

- Right sides together, matching notches, pin right side of head to upper mouth.
- Stitch right head to upper mouth.
- Right sides together, matching notches, pin right side of head to lower jaw.
- Stitch right side of head to lower jaw.

10.

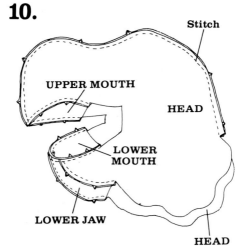

Stitch

UPPER MOUTH

HEAD

LOWER MOUTH

LOWER JAW

HEAD

- Right sides together, matching notches, pin left side of head to upper mouth.
- Stitch left side of head to upper mouth.
- Right sides together, matching notches, pin left side of head to lower jaw.
- Stitch left side of head to lower jaw.
- Right sides together, matching notches, pin lower mouth to right and left sides of head and lower jaw.
- Stitch lower mouth in place.
- Right sides together, matching notches, pin right and left side of head together.
- Stitch head pieces together.

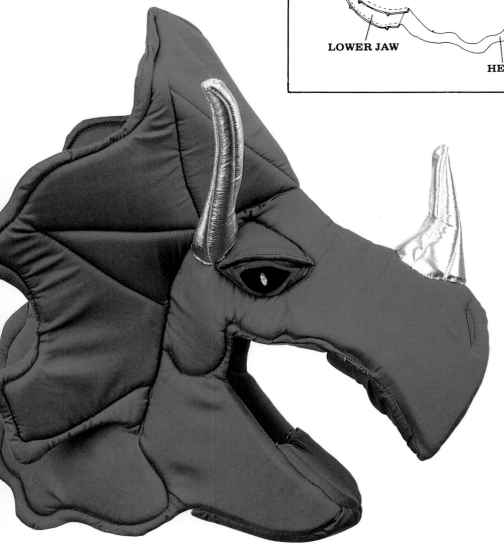

11.

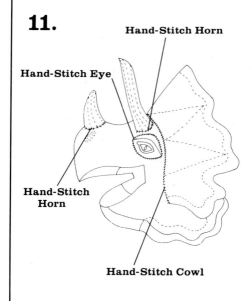

Hand-Stitch Horn

Hand-Stitch Eye

Hand-Stitch Horn

Hand-Stitch Cowl

- Turn head assembly right side out.
- Pin cowl to head along dashed line.
- Hand-stitch cowl to head.
- Hand-stitch horns to head as marked on pattern.
- Hand-stitch eyes to marks on head.

1. BODY

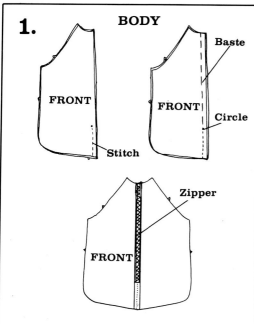

- Right sides together, pin and stitch center seam in front to circle.

- Baste center front seam together above circle. Press seam open. On inside, center closed zipper face down over basted seam with top stop ⅞" (21 cm.) from upper edge. Baste through all thicknesses—tape and fabric. On outside, stitch ¼" (6 mm.) from center seam with a zipper foot. Remove basting.

2.

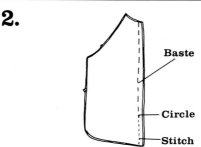

- Right sides together, matching notches, pin and stitch center seam in front lining to circle.
- Baste seam together above circle.
- Press seam open.

3.

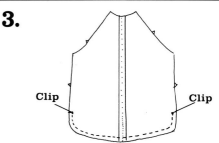

- Right sides together, matching notches, pin front lining to front.
- Stitch bottom seam, starting and stopping at circles as shown.
- Clip seams.
- Turn front right side out. Press.

4.

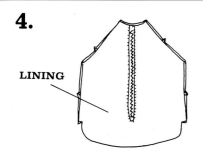

- Remove basting in front lining and hand-sew lining to zipper edge.

5.

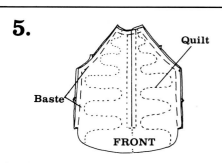

- Insert front foam pieces into casings.
- Match remaining open seams together and pin closed.
- Baste seams closed.
- Quilt front as marked on pattern. Stitch through fabric, foam, and lining.

6.

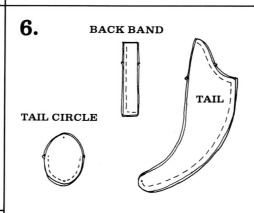

- Right sides out, matching notches, pin back band to back band lining.
- Baste as shown.
- Insert back band foam piece into fabric casing.
- Pin together remaining open seams on back band.
- Baste.
- Machine quilt following markings on pattern.
Repeat for:
  - tail band.
  - right and left tail (do not quilt).
  - tail circle (do not quilt).

7.

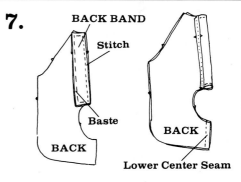

- Right sides together, matching notches, pin back band to right and left back.
- Stitch.

- Stitch lower center seam of back closed as shown.

8.

- To make dart in sleeve, fold sleeve right sides together, matching dash-dotted lines.
- Stitch and press.

9.

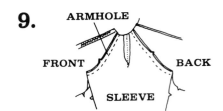

- Right sides together, matching notches and underarm and neck edges, pin sleeve to armhole edge of front and back.
- Stitch. Clip curves.

10.

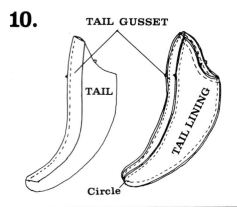

- Right sides together, matching notches, pin tail gusset to right and left tail as shown.
- Stitch.
- Right sides together, matching notches, pin remaining seam of tail together.
- Stitch.
- Trim and clip seams.
- Turn tail right side out.

11.

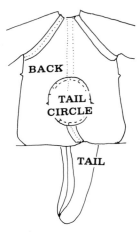

- Right sides together, matching notches, pin tail to back/back gusset opening. Baste, clipping back as necessary to aid fit. Baste.
- Pin tail circle to tail opening matching notches. Clip as necessary to aid fit. Baste.
- Stitch.

12.

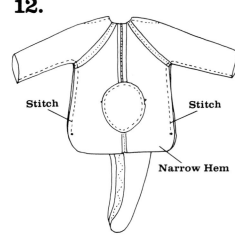

- Right sides together, matching notches and armhole seams, pin underarm and side seams together.
- Stitch.
- Narrow-hem unfinished seam on bottom of back.

13.

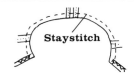

- Staystitch neck edge.

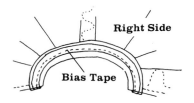

- Right sides together, pin opened double-folded bias tape to neck edge.
- Stitch.
- Trim and clip neck edge.

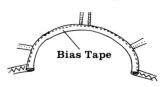

- Turn bias tape to wrong side of neck. Stitch.

14.

OPTIONAL: Appliqué fingertips on hands.
- Right sides together, matching notches, pin hand to hand lining.
- Stitch as shown.
- Clip curves and trim seams.
- Turn hand right side out.

- Insert matching foam piece into hand fabric casing.
- Quilt along markings on hand through fabric, foam, and lining.

15.

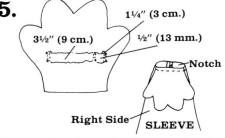

- Stitch elastic to inside (contrast color) of hand as shown.

- Right sides together, matching notches, pin hand to sleeve.
- Baste.

16.

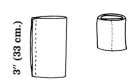

- Cut two 3″ x 7″ (8 x 18 cm.) pieces of knit ribbing.
- Right sides together, stitch ¼″ (6 mm.) from edge on ribbing.
- Fold ribbing in half with right sides facing out.

17.

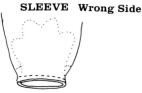

- Stretching ribbing to fit, baste to arm opening in sleeve.
- Stitch ribbing, hand, and arm opening together. Overcast seam.

- Tack ribbing to hand as shown.
- Repeat for remaining hand and sleeve.

122

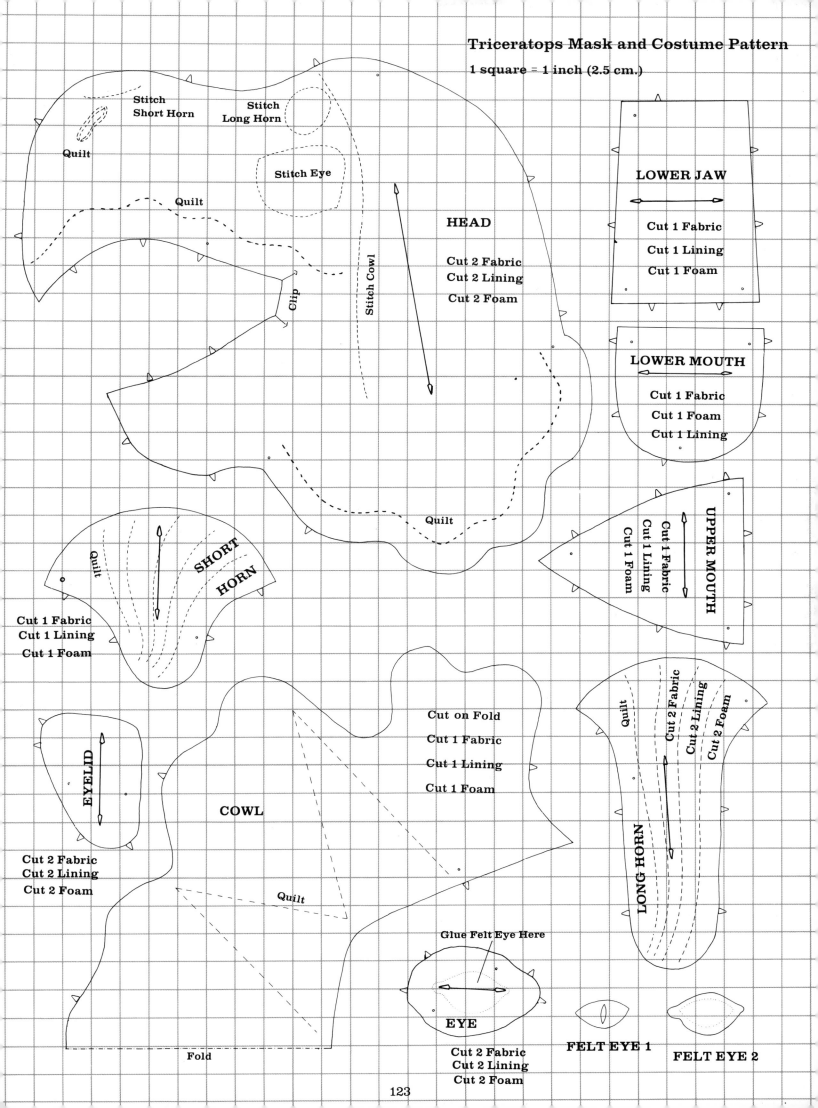

Triceratops Mask and Costume Pattern

1 square = 1 inch (2.5 cm.)

Stitch Short Horn

Stitch Long Horn

Quilt

Stitch Eye

Quilt

HEAD

Cut 2 Fabric
Cut 2 Lining
Cut 2 Foam

Clip

Stitch Cowl

Quilt

SHORT HORN

Quilt

Cut 1 Fabric
Cut 1 Lining
Cut 1 Foam

EYELID

Cut 2 Fabric
Cut 2 Lining
Cut 2 Foam

COWL

Cut on Fold
Cut 1 Fabric
Cut 1 Lining
Cut 1 Foam

Quilt

Fold

LOWER JAW

Cut 1 Fabric
Cut 1 Lining
Cut 1 Foam

LOWER MOUTH

Cut 1 Fabric
Cut 1 Foam
Cut 1 Lining

UPPER MOUTH

Cut 1 Fabric
Cut 1 Lining
Cut 1 Foam

LONG HORN

Quilt

Cut 2 Fabric
Cut 2 Lining
Cut 2 Foam

Glue Felt Eye Here

EYE

Cut 2 Fabric
Cut 2 Lining
Cut 2 Foam

FELT EYE 1

FELT EYE 2

123

Triceratops Mask and Costume Pattern

1 square = 1 inch (2.5 cm.)

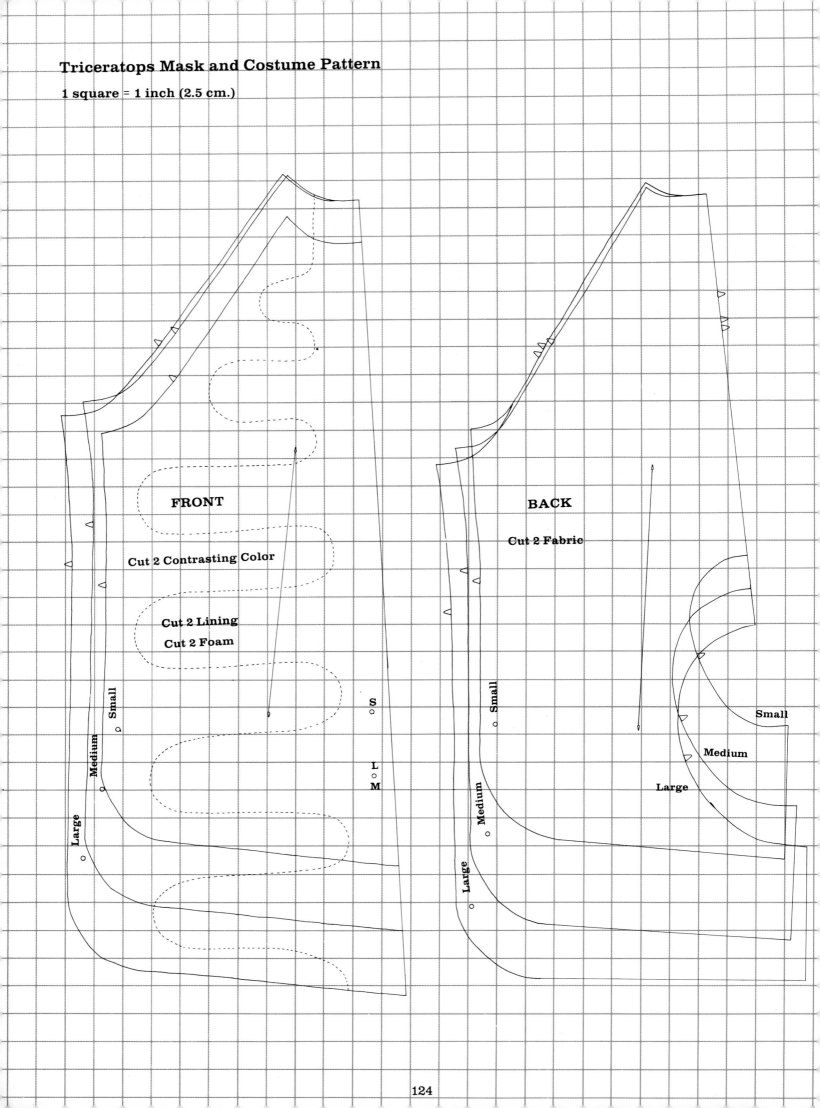

FRONT

Cut 2 Contrasting Color

Cut 2 Lining

Cut 2 Foam

Small

Medium

Large

S

L

M

BACK

Cut 2 Fabric

Small

Medium

Large

Small

Medium

Large

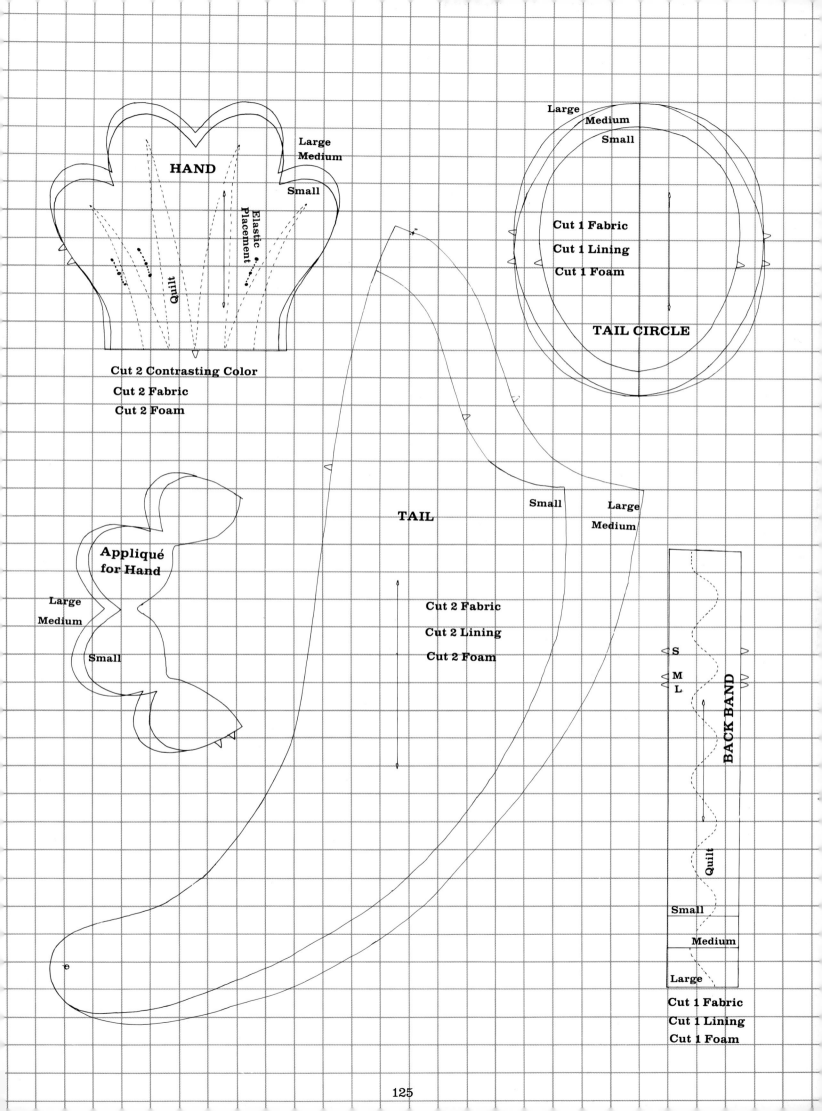

HAND

Large
Medium
Small

Elastic Placement

Quilt

Cut 2 Contrasting Color

Cut 2 Fabric

Cut 2 Foam

TAIL CIRCLE

Large
Medium
Small

Cut 1 Fabric

Cut 1 Lining

Cut 1 Foam

Appliqué for Hand

Large
Medium
Small

TAIL

Small

Large
Medium

Cut 2 Fabric

Cut 2 Lining

Cut 2 Foam

BACK BAND

S
M
L

Quilt

Small

Medium

Large

Cut 1 Fabric

Cut 1 Lining

Cut 1 Foam

Triceratops Mask and Costume Pattern

1 square = 1 inch (2.5 cm.)

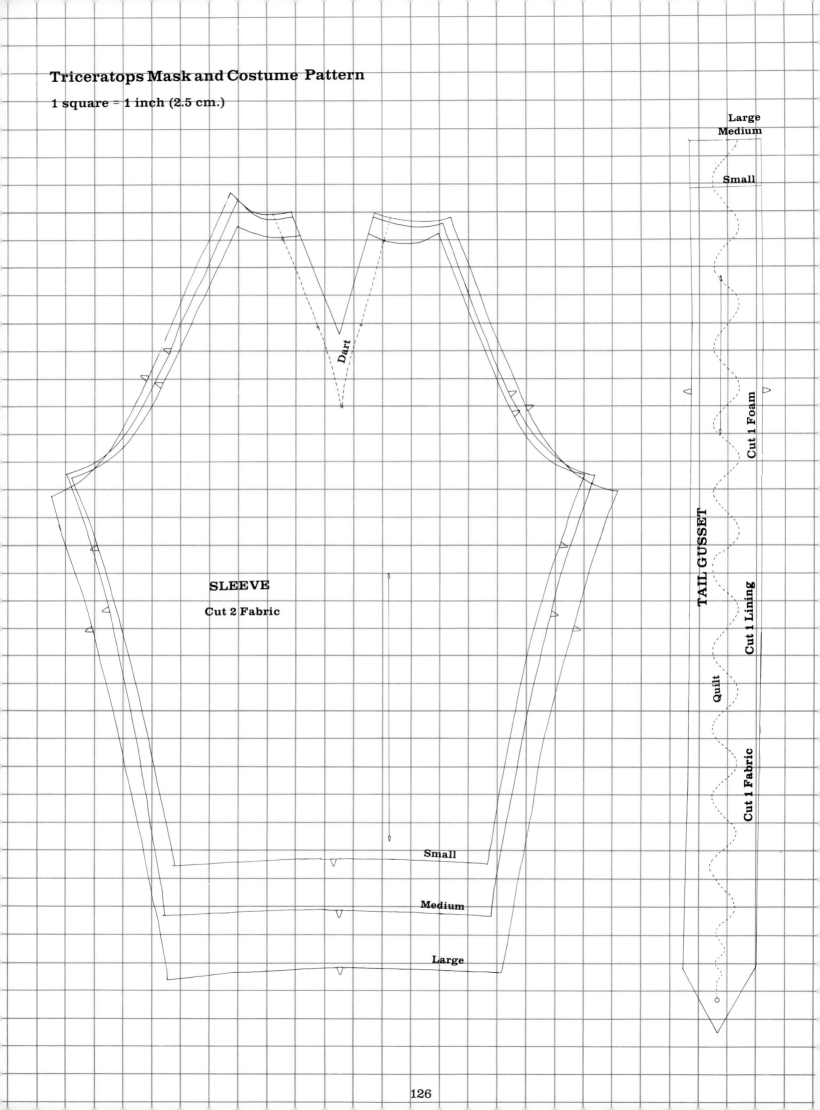

SLEEVE

Cut 2 Fabric

Dart

Small

Medium

Large

Large
Medium

Small

TAIL GUSSET

Cut 1 Foam

Cut 1 Lining

Quilt

Cut 1 Fabric

Bibliography

Basic Sewing

Brittain, Judy. *The Bantam Step-by-Step Book of Needle Craft*. New York: Bantam Books, 1979.

Eaton, Jan. *The Encyclopedia of Sewing Techniques*. Woodbury, New York: Barron's Educational Series, Inc., 1987.

Margolis, Adele. *The Encyclopedia of Sewing*. Garden City, New York: Doubleday & Company, Inc., 1987.

Surface Design

Kanzinger, Linda S. *The Complete Book of Fabric Painting*. Spokane, Washington: The Alcott Press, 1986.

Meilach, Dona Z., and Dee Managh. *Exotic Needlework*. New York: Crown Publishers, 1978.

Proctor, Richard M., and Jennifer F. Lew. *Surface Design for Fabric*. Seattle: University of Washington Press, 1984.

Dinosaurs

Benton, Michael. *The Dinosaur Encyclopedia*. New York: Simon & Schuster (Wanderer Books), 1984.

Glut, Donald F. *The Dinosaur Dictionary*. Secaucus, New Jersey: The Citadel Press, 1972.

Preiss, Byron, ed. *The Dinosaurs: A Fantastic View of a Lost Era*. New York: Bantam Books, 1981.

Pringle, Laurence. *Dinosaurs and People: Fossils, Facts, and Fantasies*. New York: Harcourt, Brace, Jovanovich, 1978.

Sattler, Helen Roney. *Dinosaurs of North America*. New York: Lothrop, Lee, and Shepard Books, 1981.

Mail-Order Sources

Many craft stores carry the eyes, joints, squeakers, and growlers that can bring a dinosaur to life. If they are not available locally, they can be ordered by mail from a number of companies, including the following:

Edinburgh Imports, Inc.
P.O. Box 722
Woodland Hills, CA 91365
(800) Edinbrg

Mimi's Books and Supplies
P.O. Box 662-C10
Point Pleasant, NJ 08742
(201) 899-0804

Newark Dressmaker Supply
6473 Ruch Road
P.O. Box 2448
Lehigh Valley, PA 18001
(215) 837-7500

Standard Doll Co.
23-83 31st Street
Long Island City, NY 11105
(800) 54DOLLS

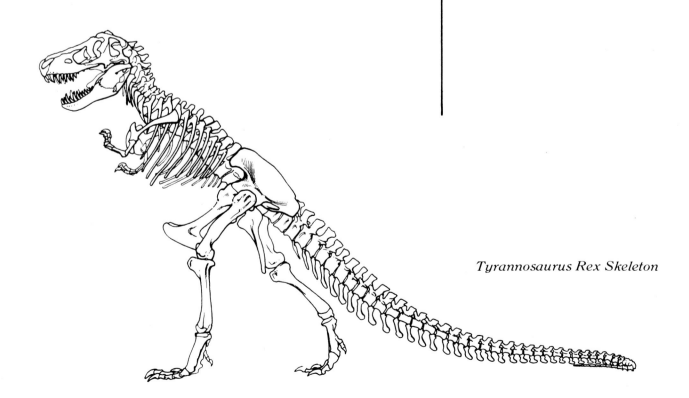

Tyrannosaurus Rex Skeleton

Index

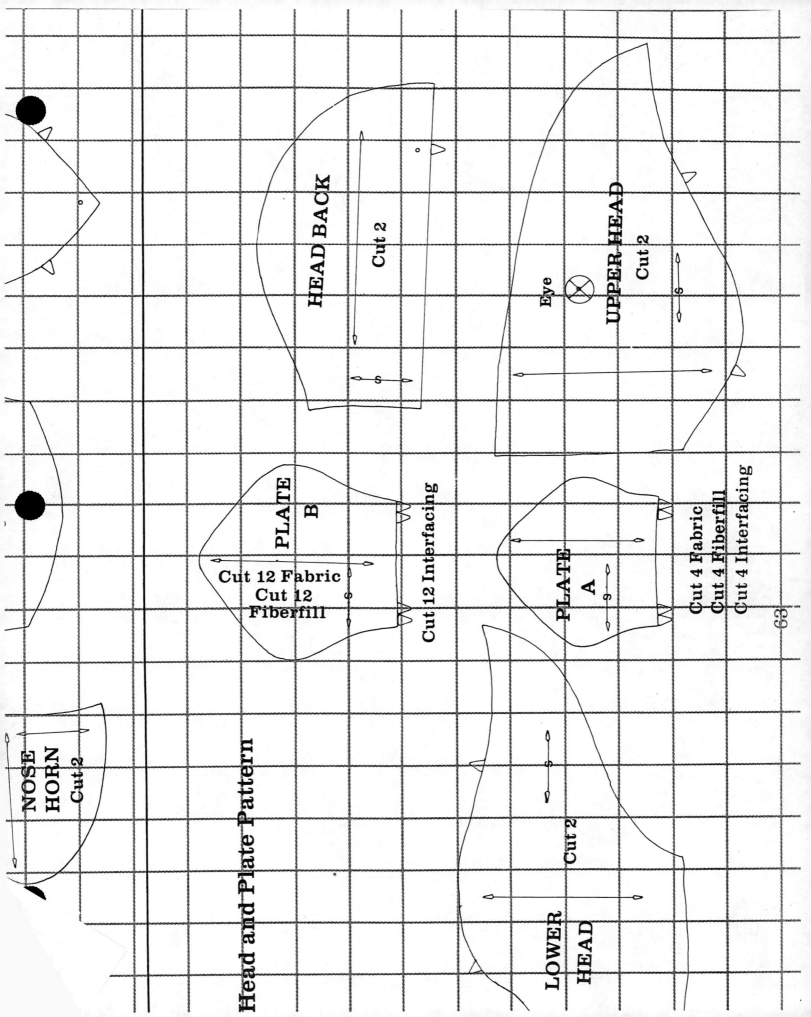

Head and Plate Pattern

NOSE HORN
Cut 2

HEAD BACK
Cut 2

UPPER HEAD
Eye ⊗
Cut 2

PLATE B
Cut 12 Fabric
Cut 12 Fiberfill
Cut 12 Interfacing

PLATE A
Cut 4 Fabric
Cut 4 Fiberfill
Cut 4 Interfacing

LOWER HEAD
Cut 2

63

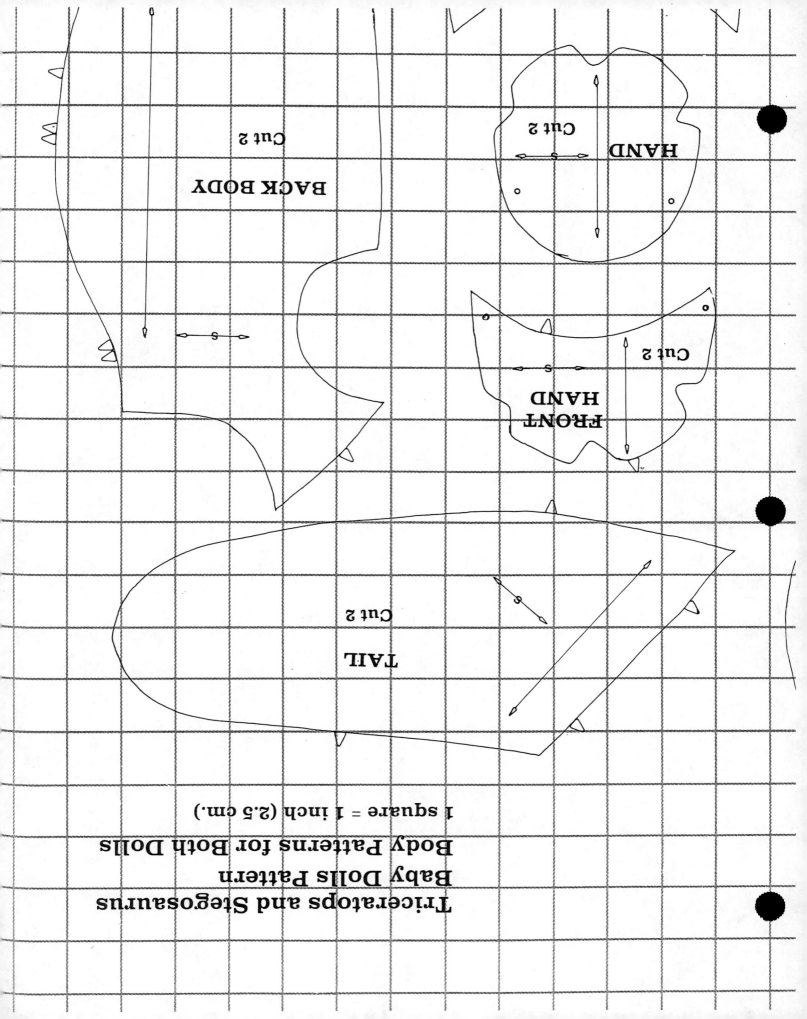

HAND
Cut 2

BACK BODY
Cut 2

FRONT HAND
Cut 2

TAIL
Cut 2

1 square = 1 inch (2.5 cm.)

Body Patterns for Both Dolls
Baby Dolls Pattern
Triceratops and Stegosaurus

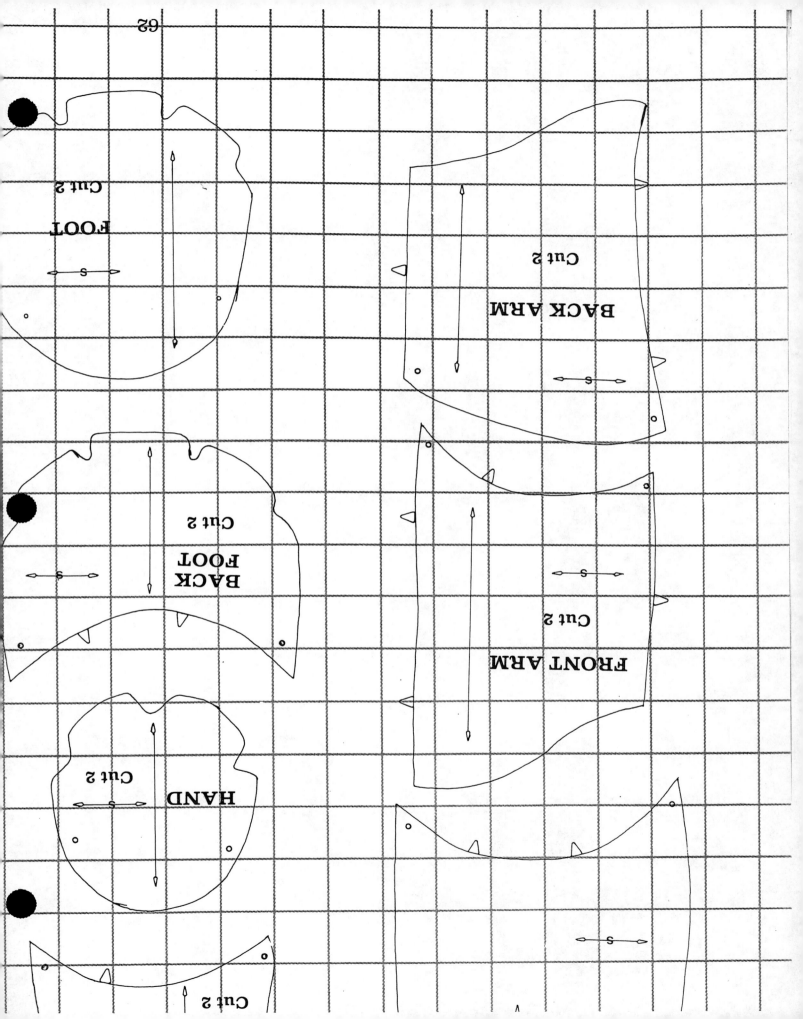

62

FOOT
Cut 2

BACK ARM
Cut 2

BACK FOOT
Cut 2

FRONT ARM
Cut 2

HAND
Cut 2

Cut 2

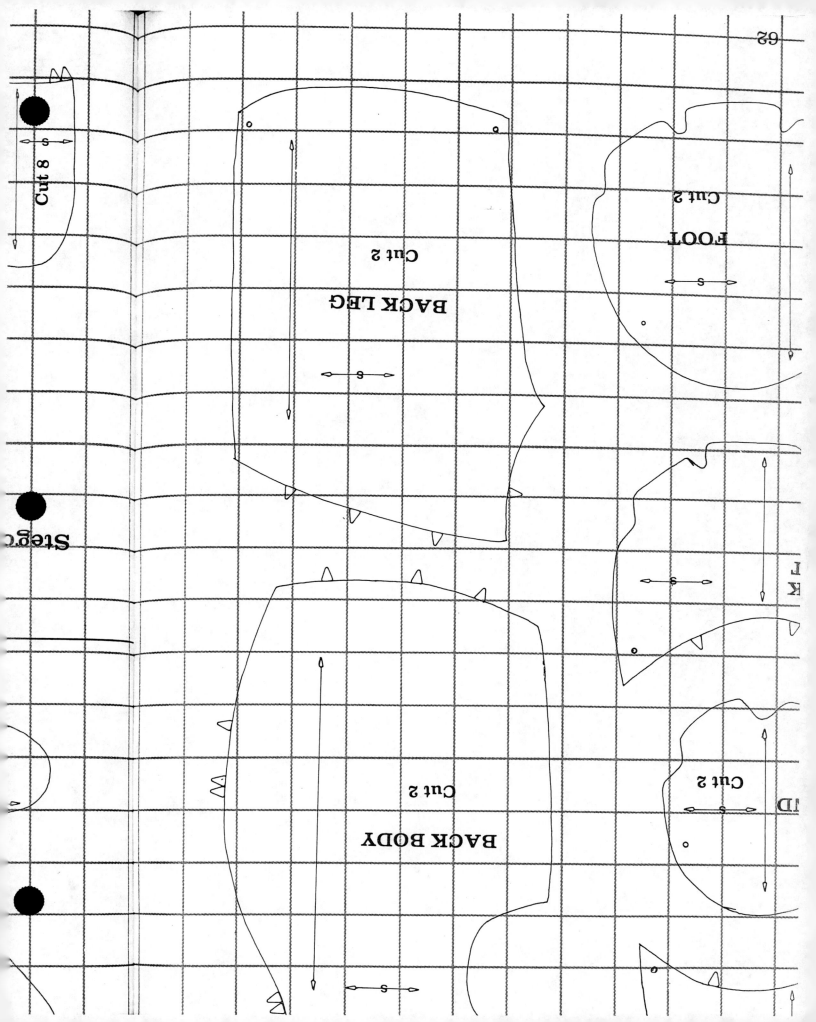

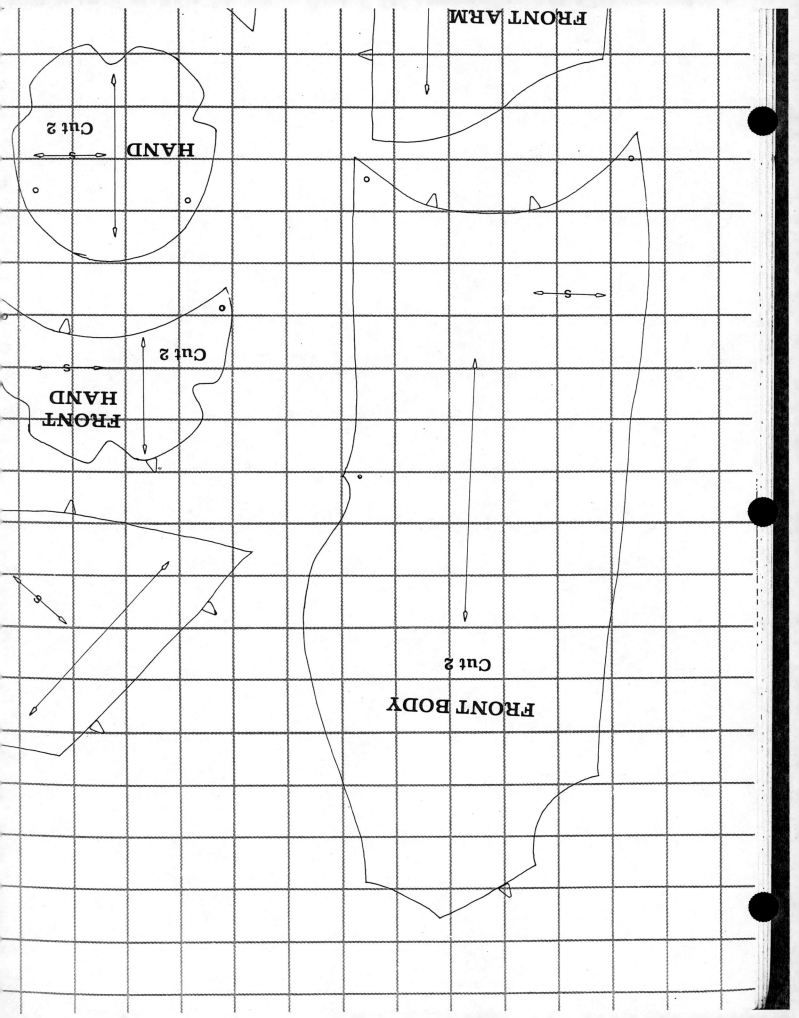

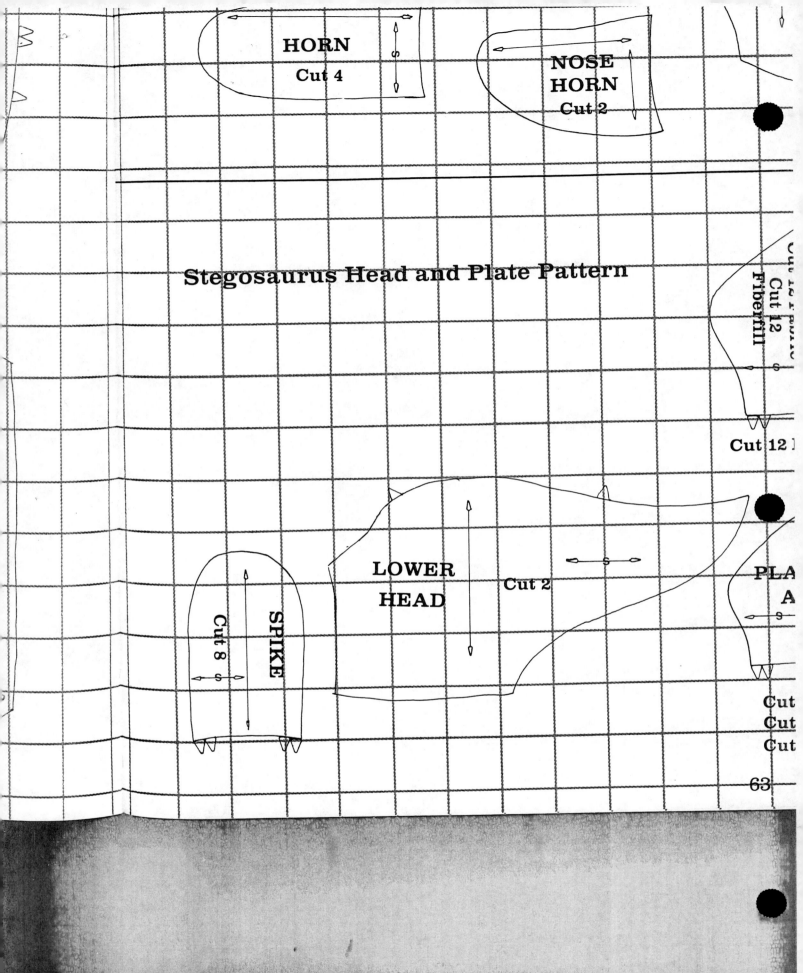

Stegosaurus Head and Plate Pattern

HORN
Cut 4

NOSE HORN
Cut 2

Cut 12
Fiberfill

Cut 12

SPIKE
Cut 8

LOWER HEAD
Cut 2

PLA
A

Cut
Cut
Cut